I0130769

Ancient Maya Ceramic Economy in the Belize River Valley Region

Petrographic analyses

Kay S. Sunahara

BAR International Series 2018
2009

Published in 2016 by
BAR Publishing, Oxford

BAR International Series 2018

Ancient Maya Ceramic Economy in the Belize River Valley Region

ISBN 978 1 4073 0593 6

© KS Sunahara and the Publisher 2009

The author's moral rights under the 1988 UK Copyright,
Designs and Patents Act are hereby expressly asserted.

All rights reserved. No part of this work may be copied, reproduced, stored,
sold, distributed, scanned, saved in any form of digital format or transmitted
in any form digitally, without the written permission of the Publisher.

BAR Publishing is the trading name of British Archaeological Reports (Oxford) Ltd.
British Archaeological Reports was first incorporated in 1974 to publish the BAR
Series, International and British. In 1992 Hadrian Books Ltd became part of the BAR
group. This volume was originally published by Archaeopress in conjunction with
British Archaeological Reports (Oxford) Ltd / Hadrian Books Ltd, the Series principal
publisher, in 2009. This present volume is published by BAR Publishing, 2016.

Printed in England

BAR

PUBLISHING

BAR titles are available from:

BAR Publishing
122 Banbury Rd, Oxford, OX2 7BP, UK
EMAIL   info@barpublishing.com
PHONE   +44 (0)1865 310431
FAX   +44 (0)1865 316916
www.barpublishing.com

ABSTRACT

Ancient Maya ceramic economy during the Late to Terminal Classic Period (800-900 A.D.) is the focus of this book. I employed ceramic thin section petrology, raw materials sourcing, and contextual archaeological analyses. Samples from a variety of excavated sites in the Belize River Valley region were included in this study: Pacbitun, Cahal Pech, Baking Pot, El Pilar, Xunantunich, Blackman Eddy, Floral Park, and Ontario Village.

Standardized petrofabric descriptions enabled the definition of distribution spheres for the ceramics. My study used intersite comparison of distributional patterning to explore issues such as the scale, integration and disposition of the ceramic economy. A number of economic models were used heuristically to examine the possible meaning of the distributional patterning observed.

I propose that ancient Maya economic systems were much more complex than have been suggested to date. I suggest a hierarchy of sites existed. This hierarchy was a framework that supported a diversity of distributive networks or spheres signifying varying degrees of economic involvement on the part of a number of sites or communities.

ACKNOWLEDGEMENTS

This book is based on research done for my doctoral dissertation in Anthropology at the McMaster University in Hamilton, Ontario, Canada. The Department of Anthropology at McMaster University, the School of Graduate Studies and the McMaster Graduate Student Association liberally provided fieldwork and travel funding. David Pendergast was instrumental in helping me gain access to Royal Ontario Museum facilities. I would like to acknowledge the entire staff of the former Near Eastern and Asian Civilizations department and current Department of World Cultures, of the Royal Ontario Museum for providing a wonderful environment in which to do my analyses, writing and editing.

I would like to thank Paul Healy, Richard Leventhal, Wendy Ashmore, Anabel Ford, James Garber, Jamie Awe, all of whom enthusiastically allowed me to sample ceramics from their field research projects for my research. The Belize Department of Archaeology allowed me to conduct my investigations and approved a number of export permits, special thanks to Jaime Awe and Allan Moore. I thank David Magaña for sharing his knowledge and samples of modern pottery raw materials sources in the Belize River Valley area. Lisa LeCount, Cynthia Robins, Sam Connell of the Xunantunich Archaeological Project helped me by providing information on their work. Bob and Nettie Jones of Eva's Restaurant are acknowledged for providing hearty meals and most importantly information and contacts in the Cayo District. Peter Zubrzyki of Pacz Hotel helped me collect raw materials samples, and generously provided transport and housing in times of need. Jennifer Piehl, David Lee, Jim Aimers and Allan Moore helped me gather sherds and information from excavations at Baking Pot. Holley Moyes, Cameron Griffith and Christophe Helmke facilitated my gathering of raw materials samples from the Roaring Creek and surrounding caves.

Many thanks also to my supervisor, Laura Finsten, who patiently urged me, ever onwards. I sincerely thank Elizabeth Graham for her early input into my research and for sitting on my comprehensive exam committee. I thank Aubrey Cannon for his "get to the point" approach that pushed me to clearly express myself. Robert Mason was a supportive teacher and thoughtful committee member without whom I would never have been able to do this research.

Invaluable friends and colleagues have all spent countless hours helping with inventories, database work, proofreading and providing inspiration and conversation. Thank you to Patricia Austin, Jennifer Babbs, Shannon Coyston, Ruth Edelstein, Cathy Friesen and Mirka Tzilivakis.

My partner, Richard Meadows has been a source of strength and purpose for me over a long and winding path filled with many surprises. Thanks also to my daughter Emi whose bright face provides me with my daily motivation.

My parents, Walter and Yoshiko Sunahara, have seen me through everything. I cannot begin to enumerate nor thank them for their unfailing support of me in both life and career. To Walter, who taught me the meaning of perseverance, will power and diplomacy, and to Yoshiko who taught me how to knock on a door and take a chance, I dedicate this work.

TABLE OF CONTENTS

Chapter

1. RESEARCH OBJECTIVES

2.   MODELS FOR ANCIENT MAYA ECONOMIES

3.   RESEARCH METHODOLOGY

7. CONCLUSION

LIST OF FIGURES

LIST OF TABLES

Research Objectives

Introduction

The central goal of the present study is to explore the structure and operation of ancient Maya economies of the Late Classic Period (A.D. 700-900) through an examination of the processes underlying the distribution of ceramic goods within the Belize River Valley. The Belize River Valley was a major subregion of lowland Maya Classic Period occupation and has been studied intensively by archaeologists for several decades. Additionally, a firm typology of ceramic types has been well established for the subregion. These factors serve as a necessary basis for the type of study I have undertaken. Following a careful selection of ceramic sherds from a variety of contexts within recently excavated sites of the Belize River Valley, I performed petrographic analysis characterization as a means of exploring two main issues: (1) whether or not individual communities produced their own pottery from nearby resources, or instead, participated in a wider intra-valley exchange sphere; and, (2) whether or not these communities participated in the importation of finished ceramics from regions beyond Belize.

By characterizing the mineralogical compositions of the sherds in my sample, and then comparing these petrofabric types to the mineralogical composition of raw materials samples collected from the Belize River Valley and to geological maps of the region, I was able to address the two central research questions. Through subsequent analyses and interpretations, ceramic distribution patterns as traced through petrographic analyses were used in conjunction with contextual archaeological information to aid in reconstructing pottery distribution spheres among Late Classic period settlements of the Belize River Valley. Evidence for extraregional interaction among these sites and polities beyond the Maya lowlands, (derived from the examination of ceramic petrofabric,) was also found (and is presented in this study). These analyses and the derived results allow me to challenge certain traditional models of ancient Maya economy and present a new approach to understanding the role of ceramics in economic processes.

Although ceramics represent only one component of ancient economies, they are found in a wide spectrum of archaeological contexts including burials, refuse middens and construction fill of all architectural structures. Most importantly, ceramics were used by the ancient Maya in a variety of economic contexts. In domestic contexts ceramics were used for food preparation, storage and consumption. In social contexts ceramic vessels were exchanged among families and socio-political elites within and among sites and regions as tokens of affiliation and alliance. Ceramics would also have been used as containers in the trade of other goods such as salt. The wide use of ceramics in these various economic contexts makes them an ideal artifact category through which to examine ancient Maya economy.

My study attempts to examine economy from a holistic perspective by looking at ceramics from the fullest possible spectrum of contexts: modest house mounds on the periphery of sites to monumental buildings at the site core. The widest possible range of contexts was sought so that the sample would be representative of each site's petrofabric repertoire.

The definition of ceramic mineralogical composition in my study allows me to investigate economic distribution issues by differentiating ceramics according to their raw materials (and their possible source), composition, and depositional context. Thus, it is possible to identify what ceramics were made of, suggest where they came from and explore the possible significance of where they ended up.

Important questions regarding ancient Maya ceramic economies such as distributional patterning and the mechanisms resulting in that patterning have not been addressed by the type-variety typologies that are most commonly the sole use to which ceramics have been put in Maya archaeology. The type-variety method, currently the standard in ceramic analysis in the Maya area, is more suited to the construction of regional and local chronological sequences (Sinopoli 1991:53). Questions concerning the organization of ceramic distribution, including how these features contribute to the formation of economic structures and the framework of ancient Maya communities, require approaches other than type-variety. Based on this assessment, my study will use petrographic analysis in concert with contextual analysis to examine ceramic distributional patterning and its significance to ancient Maya economy. Variations in ceramic petrofabrics and their distributions will be able to demonstrate whether communities were making pottery from locally available materials or whether they were obtaining pottery from other centralized manufacturing centres. For example, in the former case, I would expect to see a number of petrofabrics using locally sourced raw materials with a limited distribution area; in the latter instance I would predict that petrofabrics would be more homogenous across the wider region of the Belize River Valley. In addition to the brief overview of previous economic research provided in the following section in this chapter, I present specific expectations and predictive models based on a variety of economic models that are developed in greater detail in Chapter Two: Models for Ancient Maya Economies. In Chapter Two I assess various economic models and discuss the predicted distributional patterning implied by each. I use concepts such as distribution spheres, models such as market economies, "inward looking" and "outward looking" economic systems to evaluate Maya economic systems in the context of the Belize River Valley in the Late Classic Period. These models are tested in my study. As such, these perspectives from economic anthropology will be central to the analysis and interpretation of results from my study.

While focused on prehispanic lowland Maya society, this study represents a synthesis of archaeological and archaeometric methodologies using anthropological theory to unite two, often disparate, perspectives. This is done by taking evidence generated by an archaeometric method (in this case ceramic petrology) and using it to test anthropological distributional models with a following appraisal of the results in light of what they may suggest about the economic organization of specific archaeological communities.

Previous Research on Maya Ceramic Economy

Archaeological research into ancient Maya economic organization has traditionally focused on theories concerning long distance trade of sourceable materials, such as obsidian. Rice (1987a: 77) has observed that most often economic organization on a regional level has been characterized as the relationship between centres of elite activity and the buffer zones that provided material resources. Past research, however, has focused heavily on elite activities to the exclusion of non-elite activities. The socio-economic workings of a significant portion of Maya society, such as those who would have inhabited these vast regional buffer areas, has been the subject of little exploration. As a linked outcome, Rice (1987a: 85) suggests that Mayanists have analyzed their data from a purely political perspective, considering how economic systems could have been made to fit into radiating hierarchies or dendritic models of political structures often based on interpretations of settlement patterning. Blanton (1983:51) observes that "...archaeologists interested in early civilizations have tended to devote most of their efforts to comprehending the evolution of centralized political forms..." instead of focusing on

economic structures. The body of work on prehispanic economies is limited; however, there are some important examples to note.

Investigations at the lowland Maya sites of Palenque (Rands 1967:137-151) and Tikal (Fry 1980:3-18) have suggested that ceramic production was not necessarily concentrated in large centres. Rather, there may have been specialization in the production of particular ceramic types at individual satellite communities (Ball 1993:244; Rice 1987b:537). This type of community specialization is evidenced in the ethnographic record of Highland Guatemala (Reina and Hill 1978) and has been implied by regional studies of ceramic production in other Mesoamerican contexts, such as at La Mixtequilla in Veracruz, Mexico (Curet 1993) and in the Valley of Oaxaca, especially during the Late Postclassic (Blanton, Kowalewski, Feinman and Finsten 1981:102). At Matacapan in Veracruz, Mexico, Santley, Arnold and Pool (1989:121) have observed that although certain ceramic production locales did not exclusively manufacture set assemblages of vessels, there still was an emphasis in particular wares and forms from area to area.

Preliminary examinations of Maya ceramics from the Late Classic Period (A.D. 700-900) have suggested two different models of economic organization (Rice 1987a:79). The "Inward Looking" model postulates that production and distribution were centralized at major civic-ceremonial centres. The bulk of economic activity would have been organized and administered through these centres and would consequently be nucleated around these sites. Intra-site homogeneity would characterize the ceramic assemblage. The degree of administrative involvement and control is a key variable in this situation. For the "Inward Looking" model, administrative involvement is high with much control being exerted over the distribution of goods. Conversely, the "Outward Looking" model proposes that there is great variability among assemblages of local communities who have interdependent relationships of exchange with one another. This model also postulates that such economic ties are not oriented to major civic-ceremonial centres. In contrast, the level of administrative involvement is low in the "Outward Looking" model. On a production level, the context of ceramic manufacture has been suggested to be one of primarily "... low-level specialization and redistributive mechanism(s) probably based on kin relation" (Rice 1987a:77). This characterization is similar to what has been termed a household or cottage industry (Santley, Arnold and Pool 1989:109; Sinopoli 1991:98-99).

When attempting to study distributive mechanisms in an economy, the unit of a single site is restrictive and does not provide sufficient data to be able to discuss broader economic processes. My examination of Maya ceramics adds to the rather small number of studies employing scales of analysis larger than a single site. By incorporating a multi-site approach toward ceramic analysis in my research strategy, I can evaluate hypotheses regarding mechanisms of distribution. Few studies have sought to clarify economic relationships among sites in a region or subregion. I draw my evidence from a sample of several Belize River Valley sites of differing size and complexity in order to illuminate inter-site and subregional distribution patterns.

The results of my investigation provide a case example contributing to the ongoing debate surrounding the nature of ceramic distribution in prehispanic Mesoamerica. This debate is concerned with determining to what extent, if at all, there was centralized control over production and distribution. For the Classic Period, McAnany (1992:99) argues for a "... pluralistic economy in which the household scale of production intermeshed with larger political forces...." In the Yanamarca Valley of Peru Costin and Earle (1989) observe that Inka conquest effected little change in commoner household assemblages; however, local Wanka elites were seen to be affected having to "... adopt specifically Inka stylistic referents to status and power" (Costin and Earle 1989:711). It is suggested that Wanka elites experienced a loss of economic control due to an imperial tribute system. I ask, what was the distributional patterning for the Belize River Valley and what does this imply about its economy in the Late Classic? Ceramic material from contexts as small as house mound groupings located on the periphery of centres, as well as samples from the central precincts of sites, are examined to characterize the broadest spectrum of distribution. These economic issues are considered in greater depth in Chapter 2.

Ceramic Petrology in this Study

The investigative tool of ceramic petrology provides me with the necessary data to discuss distributional patterning. Additionally, an improved understanding of the material composition of ceramics clarifies the identification of resources procured and utilized by ancient Maya potters. Were certain types of temper used in the production of specific kinds of vessels such as water jugs, serving vessels, and cooking pots? Were tempers chosen for characteristic technical properties, expediency or both?

Historically, archaeologists in the Maya area have been able to trace the development of pottery though time. They have constructed regional and local chronological sequences from ceramics, and laid the essential foundations for our understanding of the development of Maya society. A typology based on petrographic identification of the non-plastic inclusions in ceramic bodies seeks to examine issues I have outlined, as these differ from those addressed by the type-variety system to date. Typologies produced from petrographic investigations need not threaten the systems in place as Jones (1986) suggests. Petrofabric analysis has the potential to enhance the type-variety systems that have been constructed.

By using the technique of petrographic analysis, this study identifies variations in the use of non-plastic inclusions, including temper, in the ceramics sampled. Temper is a component in the make-up of a ceramic fabric that is purposefully added to the clay improving its workability, strength when fired, porosity and, at times, a vessel's surface finish. Under this definition non-plastic inclusions may or may not be termed as temper. Non-plastic inclusions may be naturally present in the clay. My study of non-plastic inclusions will not in itself be able to pinpoint the location of clay sources and this is beyond the defined scope of this current investigation. To do this, techniques such as neutron activation analysis and scanning electron microscopy need to be used. The uses of these other archaeometric measures are a consideration after accessing the results of this petrographic study.

Potential Contributions

On a general level, a study of ceramic economy contributes to understanding of the development of economic systems within early state societies. Ceramic material has been used in studies seeking to define the role of changing economic systems in the development of early state societies. In the Near East, Wattenmaker (1994:105-109) associates increasing ceramic standardization and craft specialization with political centralization. By using the unit of labour instead of ceramics, "transformations in the mode of production" from kin to household-based to tributary and state organized have been identified by La Lone (1994) as having been linked to the success of the Inka as an empire. My investigation into economy through the use of ceramics augments the literature on this subject in the Maya region. The illumination of economic developments through my research, using ceramics from a range of contexts, contributes significantly to settlement investigations by providing an integrated viewpoint. Maya archaeology has traditionally focused on the excavation of elite contexts in association with monumental architecture (palace and temple structures) located at the core of Maya sites. Recent trends in settlement research have prompted the investigation of commoner or non-elite contexts (house mounds), usually located in peripheral zones of a given site. Often studies of these two sections of the site, core and periphery, are considered in near isolation with limited cross-referencing of results and implications. My investigation provides articulation between these two sets of archaeological data, thereby potentially permitting a more holistic view of Maya culture and promoting the abandonment of a dichotomy founded largely on a division in archaeological research methodology.

In ancient Maya ceramic studies technical analyses such as ceramic petrography have traditionally been viewed as irreconcilable with the type-variety form of classification (Sheppard 1956:315-316). I propose to demonstrate that this adversarial situation need not necessarily be the case.

As I have stated, my study will contribute to the expansion of the use of petrographic information to address specific questions about economy different from those stylistic and chronometric issues that concern type-variety typologies. An examination of ceramic distribution spheres in this manner will contribute to the development of additional classificatory criteria that can be used in ceramic analyses.

The examination of ceramics to obtain a clearer understanding of the organization of ancient Maya economies will have significance in other facets of inquiry. Certainly this approach will lend further support to the growing, and essential, shift towards interdisciplinary research. Too often information and conclusions resulting from archaeometric analyses have been difficult for archaeologists to access due to the specialized language involved in presentation of the data and conclusions. This inaccessibility too often results in a marginalization of such results in the formulation of archaeological interpretations, particularly those in the anthropological tradition (De Atley and Bishop 1991:365-366). This study will attempt to clarify and increase the area of interface between material scientists and anthropological archaeologists.

Summation

Through the examination of role ceramics played in a prehispanic early state economy, the results of this project make a direct contribution to economic anthropology, as well as to the archaeological analysis of ceramics. Ceramics have been analyzed here from the perspective of socio-economy and are used to address research problems that involve something other than the construction of a relative local chronology. There is an urgent need to push the use of ceramics beyond the mere construction of typologies for typological sake, and my work represents one attempt to do so. It is hoped that studies using ceramic petrography in the Maya area will multiply. My research seeks to encourage the use of this technique by demonstrating its utility in addressing archaeological concerns of early state economy in one subregion of the Maya region.

Chapter Overview

In Chapter Two I discuss current thinking about economic organization in the Maya area. Part of the discussion is concerned with forms of ceramic evidence; however, the chapter does encompass broader perspectives and different types of data categories, thereby setting the stage for this research and providing the basis for interpretive comparisons between the results of this study and those of other researchers.

Chapter Three focuses on research methodology. I describe the research region and discuss the units of analysis and why they were selected. Descriptions of sites included in my study are presented providing

specific archaeological context to the investigation. A detailed discussion of sample contexts and lists of the samples from each site accompany each site description. The progression of my field research and sampling procedures are also outlined in this chapter.

Analytical methods are the topic of Chapter Four. Ceramic petrology and the different variables involved in its archaeological application are discussed. Additionally, petrographic concepts and terms such as "granulometry" and "textural analysis" are defined along with a discussion of their relevance to my work. The rationale and coverage range of the raw materials sampling program I conducted is also presented in this chapter.

Accompanied by an explanation of nomenclature, descriptions of petrofabric groups generated by this research are to be found in Chapter Five. Descriptions involve mineralogical identification, as well as observation of abundance and granulometry. Preliminary insights into the significance of each petrofabric group introduced here to lay the basis for in-depth discussion in the next chapter. This chapter also includes the results and discussion of the raw materials sampling program that I conducted.

Chapter Six provides analysis and interpretation of the petrofabrics presented in the previous chapter. Specific data on the examined sample are presented here to aid in the evaluation of results. The results of petrographic analysis are discussed from an intersite and regional viewpoint with an emphasis on what has been learned about the nature of Late Classic Maya economies in the Belize River Valley region through this study.

A summary of conclusions and an assessment of the significance of research findings are provided in Chapter Seven. Additionally, further questions raised by the investigation are presented and explored in this final chapter.

2

Models for Ancient Maya Economies

Introduction

This chapter explores proposed models of ancient Maya economies to provide a comparative framework in which to interpret the results of this study. It must be acknowledged that models are idealized structures representing specific aspects of the phenomena they are trying to explain. By their very nature models are hard pressed to incorporate all the multifarious aspects of anything as complex as an economy. Given this situation, the value derived from a given model is not so much what it is, but how it is applied, or operationalized in a specific scenario (Isaac 1996:329-330). Models aid in the interpretation of archaeological data and help us understand the societies, people and circumstances that produced the archaeological record. The specific aim in my discussion is to consider distributional models and how they may be applied to understand attributes of the economic system that was in operation during the Late Classic period in the Belize River Valley area. While some of the discussion revolves around ceramics, included are relevant works that have examined the issues of inter-site and regional economic activities involving other classes of goods with particular emphasis on investigation in the southern Maya lowlands and Belize.

Historically, there has been a general lack of treatment by Mayanists of economic issues. Culbert (1977:511) notes this in his discussion of Maya development and collapse. McAnany (1989a:1) voices similar sentiments in her introduction to a volume on Maya economies in Belize. Studies have generally treated economy on an implicit level without detailed explanations of assumed attributes. Often, assumptions have been made about ancient economies that have relied on extrapolations from reconstructions of political organization based primarily on glyphic information with supporting settlement and environmental data. Inferences about economies have been generated in light of proposed structures of political organization. In these studies, an explicit definition of economic models and their traits is difficult to identify. A small but growing number of select investigations have focused unambiguously on factors of production and distribution by examining different commodities and their role in economic networks. In these cases, larger economic structures are discussed as the matrix within which particular artifacts circulate. Readily provenienced materials such as obsidian and chert have been popular subjects of these studies. Wider use of archaeometric methods has enabled the definition of origin and tracing of movement for artifacts. Based on this information models have been generated and tested to articulate economic systems. It is this type of work that will be considered in this chapter.

Approaches to Economic Organization

A growing body of research on ancient Maya economies focuses on specific artifacts recovered in excavations. The application of analytical methods and the addition of archaeometric techniques have fostered detailed research on the role played by lithics and ceramics in Maya economies. A host of studies on trade such as Sabloff and Rathje's (1973, 1975) examination of Postclassic trade at the island of Cozumel; Friedel's (1978) work at Cerros describing maritime trade in the Formative period; and Spence's (1996) exploration of the role of long distance trade of Teotihuacan green obsidian in the Maya region, may all be considered to be similar to this approach. The following discussion examines specific studies that describe economic models and address issues of distributional patterning.

The significance of regional and local variation and availability of resources is an important factor in the reconstruction of economic systems. Graham (1987) highlights this in her study of resource diversity in Belize. Whereas resources were previously considered to be uniform across the lowland Maya area, significant variability has been identified in lithic resources, clays, and soils in the lowland environment. Graham (1987:753, 763) sees the recognition of this variability by archaeologists as not only important in the reconstruction of local exchange networks, but also integral to an understanding of larger socioeconomic processes such as culture change through trade. The redefinition of the Maya lowlands as heterogeneous in resource distribution and diversity has become apparent to archaeologists who have performed lithic and ceramic studies identifying production areas, tracing distributional patterning of artifacts, and modeling economy.

Lithics, especially obsidian, have enabled archaeologists to investigate both local and regional models of exchange. With the development and refinement of trace element analyses, using neutron activation and X-ray fluorescence, numerous studies have been performed on obsidian for the Maya area (Dreiss et al. 1993; Hammond 1972; McKillop et al. 1988; Nelson et al. 1977). The ability to find the geological origin of obsidian, differentiate among a variety of sources and thereby trace movement, has allowed archaeologists to explore issues of economy and trade with some detail.

Ceramic material has received somewhat different treatment. When examining ceramics to elucidate economic organization the majority of studies have focused on the facets of distribution and exchange rather than tracing pottery production sources since data on actual production locations have not been recovered (Rice 1987b:529). Ceramic material provenance was, and is still, problematic as actual areas of production have not been located. Research and survey strategies to this point have not focused on finding production areas that are thought to have been located away from the nuclei of civic ceremonial centres. As a result, studies of production have worked backwards from the technological aspects of pottery, and what modes of production would have been needed, to produce certain qualities, quantities and distribution of ceramic material. In many instances researchers implicitly assume that most ceramics have generally small spheres of distribution and that local level self-sufficiency was in operation. Additionally, many of these studies have centred on what have been deemed "elite" ceramics, such as polychrome painted vessels (Beaudry 1987; LeCount 1999) that comprise a select portion of ceramic assemblages of any particular area.

Market Economy Processes

McKillop (1996) presents a convincing argument for a Maya trading port at the site of Wild Cane Caye in the southern coast of Belize. High densities of obsidian found at the site have been argued to imply greater access to this non-local resource due to Wild Cane Caye's status as a trading port. The wide diversity of obsidian types, numbering six different sources revealed by trace element analyses, further support the trade port hypothesis. A regional survey found that Wild Cane Caye was well integrated within the regional economy, supplying obsidian and other trade goods to surrounding sites. Observations on the obsidian assemblage are considered in the context of other artifact classes such as ceramics and chert lithics. Additionally, evidence of salt production is used to produce a model of the integration of different regional economies through the use of maritime trade ports and long-distance trade. McKillop (1996:49-50, 52) argues against the "port-of-trade" model of Polanyi et al. (1957) where elite goods were controlled and used exclusively by elites effectively limiting regional distribution of these commodities, a scenario McKillop posits is not supported by the widespread distribution of these goods. Another model for trade, "down-the-line" exchange (Renfrew 1977), was found not to fit the distributional patterns uncovered by

McKillop's investigations. The characteristic decline in densities of non-local goods, in this case obsidian, in relation to distance from the sources, was certainly not evident for south coastal Belize. In modeling Classic and Postclassic period economies McKillop (1996:50) suggests that "... the ancient Maya were reacting to the forces of supply and demand, based on concepts of rational choice, scarcity, and maximization, even without a modern marketplace economy."

The Pulltrouser Swamp zone and adjacent sites in northern Belize, including Colha, have been the subject of a number of investigations involving the examination of chert tool production, distribution, and craft specialization (Shafer and Hester 1983; McAnany 1989c, 1991). After analysis of chert debitage from residential middens at the site of Pulltrouser Swamp, McAnany (1989c:341-342) concluded that Pulltrouser was a consumer base for chert tools produced at Colha. Debitage indicated maintenance and recycling of broken tools made of Colha chert. Chert from Colha was not directly procured for manufacture of tools at Pulltrouser; to the contrary, tools were traded in as finished products. Colha was seen to be the primary producer of chert tools with evidence of workshops (Shafer and Hester 1983:522-524) that supplied the surrounding sites of Pulltrouser Swamp, Cuello, Cerros, and Kichpanha. McAnany (1989:342) also notes slight variation in the Colha-produced tools in assemblages at different locales, suggesting that the element of consumer choice based on locally specific subsistence requirements was also an important factor in distributional patterning. Colha was the source of a supply network covering northern and coastal Belize as well as southern parts of Quintana Roo. McAnany (1989c:342) cites the works of Gibson (1986) and Moholy-Nagy (1983) to describe and extend distributional zones that supplied stemmed macroblades and "eccentric" symbolic chert implements to such distant sites as Tikal in the Peten region of Guatemala. Production centres and distribution networks operated simultaneously at many different scales and the economic significance of a site "...may not be related to the size of its pyramids, its population size, or its political importance" (McAnany 1989c:342).

Fry (1979) has analyzed the geographic distribution of serving vessels to examine modes of pottery exchange at the site of Tikal using both stylistic and technological attributes. Six different models of exchange were considered: supply zone, gift exchange, simple centralized redistribution, noncentralized marketing, complex redistribution and complex market. This typology is meant to describe the possible distributional patterning of ceramics produced by one centre. The expected patterning for each model is defined and the results of the geographical analysis are then compared. Supply zone exchange is described as one to one exchange between the producer and consumer at the place of use or production. Gift exchange is defined as simple exchange most often part of a complex web of structured exchange relationships. Simple centralized redistribution was composed of the pooling and redistribution of goods by a centrally positioned person or institution. Simple centralized marketing outlined a situation where exchange occurred via one centrally located market. Noncentralized marketing was where exchange was done through a series of small scale markets lacking any general systemization. Complex redistributive systems pooled and redistributed resources on various tiers of a hierarchy. Finally, complex markets used a hierarchically ordered host of local and regional markets of various scales to facilitate exchange.

Fry (1979:510) concludes that serving vessels were part of a complex market system with a central market and regional exchange centres. In modeling a complex market system, Fry (1979:497) describes situation where exchange occurred through an organization of hierarchically stratified sets of regional markets of differing scales. The predicted distributional patterning at a given centre would be that of widespread distribution with higher degrees of similarity among assemblages at different centres and market areas than would theoretically be found in another model such as simple centralized distribution. Ceramic assemblages at central sites would exhibit greater variety since these central sites would be the location of marketplaces drawing in ceramics from surrounding areas. Those sites considered peripheral in geographic distance would have a lesser degree of variation in their assemblages.

Expanding his analysis to a collection of sites in south-central Quintana Roo, Mexico, to compare with Tikal in Guatemala, Fry (1980) looks at many classes of pottery, including but not limited to serving vessels as in his previous study. Using the same methodology, examining slipped bowls, basins, jars and unslipped coarse jars, Fry (1980:18) again concludes that the system observed, although less centralized than might have been expected, is classifiable as a complex market system that included local distribution systems. An implication of this complex market model, craft specialization in ceramic production, is mentioned as an alternative occupational option for the large populations surrounding vast centres such as Tikal.

A Question of Scale: Local or External Factors?

Rice (1987b:532) notes that Fry's study of Tikal involved a small sustaining area surrounding the site rather than an actual geographically defined regional area. The issue of scale in economic models is important and is well illustrated by the next two models discussed, the "inward-looking" and "outward-looking" models.

Sites in the region surrounding Palenque, as well as Palenque itself, have been studied using technological (petrology and neutron activation analysis) and stylistic analyses (Rands 1967; Rands and Bishop 1980). Diagnostic properties of the pottery were analyzed and compared to clays sourced in the local vicinity. These factors were in turn correlated to stylistic and formal attributes of the pottery (Rands 1967:140-141). Economic organization is discussed with reference to two models: "inward-looking" and "outward-looking." The "inward-looking" model described an internal exchange system with nearly exclusive use of local resources and trade in local products. Pottery may have been produced at satellite sites but would have been distributed through a central market located at Palenque. This "inward-looking" model would reflect in very limited distribution of Palenque ceramics outside its bounded regional area. In contrast, the "outward-looking" model described a situation where external trade occurred regularly and exchange boundaries less defined (Rands and Bishop 1980:43).

Rands and Bishop posit that Palenque was the hub of ceramic distribution and imported ceramics from surrounding sites more than it exported its own local pottery. Craft specialization in specific vessel classes was suggested to have occurred on a community-to-community basis with each community funneling its wares through Palenque. Rands and Bishop (1980:43) acknowledge that the two models they discuss are constructs sitting at opposite ends of the spectrum and that their utility is in the contrasts they present in aid of interpreting the results of their study. Although it appeared that the investigators might favour the "inward-looking" model, final conclusions as to the nature of economic organization at Palenque and its surrounding region were reserved pending further testing of ceramic groupings. In addition, it should also be noted that the ceramic groups selected for their study were already considered to be "… indigenous to the general region" (Rands and Bishop 1980:22) at the onset of their investigation.

A smaller scale study was performed on ceramics from the site of Lubaantun, in southern Belize. Local clay samples and pottery recovered from excavations were tested using neutron activation analysis (Hammond et al. 1976). By looking at trace elements it was found that the Lubaantun ceramic assemblage was largely composed of vessels made from locally derived clays sourced within six kilometres from the site. Occasional imports from the Pasión region of Guatemala were identified in the presence of Fine Orange ceramic type. A relatively large number of tripod vessels at Lubaantun were discovered to be those also found at sites in the Belize River Valley region. It is unclear why, when referring to the Belize Valley tripod vessels, Hammond (1982:228) states "… they did not supply any economic need at Lubaantun…." Despite the tripod vessels found in frequencies too numerous to be considered elite gifts, it is suggested that an "inward-looking" model best fits the economic organization at Lubaantun. However, it may be asked whether the smaller "inward-looking" model might be imbedded within larger scale economic frameworks especially given observations made on

Belize Valley tripod vessels. It can be questioned whether either of the models alone can effectively describe the situation at Lubaantun since both assume that all types of ceramics participated in the same distributional mechanisms.

As can be seen in the previous discussion, scale is an integral issue in modeling economies. Hammond's Lubaantun study was centred on that site and ceramics tested from that site. Rands and Bishop's investigation was based on an examination of a wider geographical area, yet sites other than Palenque that were tested were already considered to be in the regional area politically controlled by Palenque. It should not be surprising that distributional patterns appear to favour an internally focused model. Studies have not succeeded in gathering appropriate data to enable the true testing of an "outward-looking" model.

Research Issues

From my evaluation of the surveyed literature, it is apparent that different scales of analysis are required to meet the challenge of researching economic organization in the Maya area. I suggest that a shift away from single site focused studies to regional scale investigations will contribute to understanding these types of processes by enabling the examination of intersite economic relationships and spheres of distribution. Researchers should be questioning the validity of generalizations about the state of ancient Maya economic organization. For instance, assumptions such as the operation of market type economic processes need to be tested. Within a regional context, detailed studies into particular aspects of economic organization, the resources, artifacts and distributional patterns are needed. Regional scales of study and resource surveys need to be included in research designs, as well as the usual settlement pattern surveys, to be able to understand local and extra-local distributional patterning.

A search for regional models against which to compare data in my study has resulted in the identification of three models of ancient Maya economic organization. Though not necessarily mutually exclusive, these models represent different aspects of current thinking on economic organization for the lowland region. There are models that have used modern marketplace economy concepts, such as the acting forces of "supply and demand" and rational choice, with centralized hierarchically controlled redistributive mechanisms. The "inward-looking" and "outward-looking" models, placed in opposition to one another, describe situations that represent different ends of a wide spectrum. The "inward-looking" model outlines a situation where there is a restricted locally controlled exchange system with localized distributional patterning. Conversely, the "outward-looking" model describes a less centrally controlled system with external contacts and a broader patterning of distribution.

The majority of studies have centred on archaeological material from one particular site and its surrounding area, often referred to as a "sustaining area." Where multiple sites are considered they are usually satellite sites of a prominent civic-ceremonial centre. It still can be said that such studies are intra-site focused when evaluating the scale at which they address economic organization. These circumscribed studies do not effectively address economic issues since these processes for complex societies, such as that of the ancient Maya, operate on a much larger scale than any single site alone. Regionally scaled studies are rare in the Maya region, but it is apparent that they are needed to enable an understanding of economic organization from a larger more truly inter-site perspective.

Model Application In This Study

My study uses petrographic analysis of ceramic material to identify distributional patterning within a regional context of eight sites in the geographic region of the Belize River Valley. The eight sites considered in this investigation range in scale from large centres with significant monumental structures to medium and small scale sites. (Detailed discussion of the sites is presented in the following chapter on research methodology.) I will use these models in a heuristic fashion to interpret and discuss attributes of the distributional patterning I have found, rather than attempting to fit the data into any particular framework. Models will provide the basis by which I consider what the distributional information suggests in terms of reconstructing ancient Maya economic organization.

3

Research Methodology

The Belize River Valley Region and Units of Analysis

As a better understanding of regional socio-economy through ceramics is the goal of this study, I found it necessary to select a research unit that would be able to support the demands of this type of investigation. A regional, multi-site approach was purposefully chosen in order to examine economic relationships among different sites. A multi-site perspective was better able to consider ceramic distribution and patterning as traced through petrographic analyses where different sites would be located near different raw materials resources. For instance, one site might be on the river's edge in walking distance of granitic sand while another site might be located in limestone foothills.

Inclusion of sites of different scales was essential to the articulation of the fullest possible spectrum of economic interactions. I hoped that phenomena such as varying levels of participation in exchange and distribution networks might be revealed in this manner. Would larger sites have the greatest number of petrofabric types regardless of surrounding raw material sources, supporting the hypothesis that they served as the hub of some redistributive mechanism or marketplace? Would smaller sites have fewer petrofabric types and also be restricted to those of local origin? These are some examples of the types of questions I wanted to be able to consider by using a regional multi-site approach.

Ideally, the region would have already been extensively surveyed, mapped and excavated. Selecting a region where only a couple of large sites were known and investigated, for example, would not facilitate the goals of this research. The Belize River Valley region has not been subject to a comprehensive full coverage survey; instead, specific sites and their peripheries have been mapped and excavated. Research based on a regional scale of analysis, although widely accepted as desirable, is only slowly being implemented in field practice in the Maya region. The units of analysis used in archaeological research in the Belize River Valley region have been single sites in isolation. With the exception of Ford (1990, 1991) and Fedick's (1988, 1989) work on the north side of the Belize River, most settlement surveys and archaeological investigations have been conducted in the immediate environs of specific centres. Full coverage surveys of certain subregional areas have started to be implemented in the Maya area; unfortunately, the results

of these studies are yet to be made accessible. This condition is largely due to research focus of investigators and the system of archaeological permit allocation.

Notwithstanding this site-centric focus, archaeological research in the Belize River Valley has flourished ever since Willey et al.'s (1965) seminal work on prehistoric settlement for this region. It was Willey's (1973:270) view that settlement patterns are the foundations upon which societies build their social systems. From this point onwards, a steady stream of archaeologists has made sites along the Belize River Valley the subject of their field research. The Belize River Valley, in comparison to other areas in the Maya region, has been widely explored and was deemed suitable for the purposes of my study.

Variable geology surrounding the Belize Valley was also a factor that made it a suitable area for my study. The underlying geology of the region is sedimentary in nature with limestones forming the bedrock. Southeast of the Belize Valley, the Mountain Pine Ridge formation represents an area of metamorphic rocks, primarily granites. The Belize River and its tributaries drain the Mountain Pine Ridge and deposit eroded sands along the riverbanks in the valley. Variable geology increases the likelihood that a number of distinct petrofabrics might be found. A range of petrofabrics would provide a better basis for determining the nature of distribution patterns that was central to my research.

An additional feature of the Belize Valley that made it appropriate for this study was that researchers using methods other than petrological analysis have studied the pottery. The definition of various ceramic types by Gifford (1976) provides a basis for dating pottery on surface and formal attributes in a type-variety typology. Of specific interest to me was the "Spanish Lookout Ceramic Sphere" a pottery complex typical of the entire region that dates to the 9th Century A.D. (Late Classic period). Spanish Lookout is described as a local ceramic tradition of the Late Classic to Terminal Classic periods (Willey, Culbert and Adams 1967:301). Researchers have suggested that the Belize Valley appears to have been part of the trend towards ceramic regionalism (Ball 1976:328); indeed, for the Late Classic, all of the sites included in my study rendered sherds from the Spanish Lookout Sphere. Previous research on ceramics in this region provided me with a basis for dating and selecting appropriate samples.

Certain other criteria also needed to be met for my research strategy. The base unit of analysis within the region would be the site in order to effectively compare ceramic assemblages and their petrofabric distributional patterning. Samples needed to be selected from a variety of sites, large, medium and small, over a regional expanse. Each site would need to have already undergone adequate investigation so as to provide contextual information for the ceramic samples. Additional logistical considerations included accessibility to the ceramic assemblages. I needed to be able to see the complete range of ceramics from each site to do the preliminary petrological survey and select samples for thin sectioning. Thus, cooperation was sought and received from a number of researchers already leading excavation projects in the region and much time was spent in their field labs and storage facilities.

A preliminary feasibility study conducted amongst researchers in the Belize Valley in 1995 showed that most archaeologists working in the region were readily willing to provide ceramic materials and share information on their sites for this study. The eight sites included in this study were: Cahal Pech, Blackman Eddy, Xunantunich, El Pilar, Floral Park, Baking Pot, Ontario Village and Pacbitun. These sites and the projects conducted therein fulfill the criteria outlined above. Moreover, they are representative of the range of site types, at least in terms of size and complexity, for the Late Classic Belize River Valley. I sought to include large and small sites in my sample to provide a sound base from which to elicit information on different spheres of ceramic distribution and thereby investigate possible patterning. Figure 3.1 on the following page is a map that features all sites in my research area in addition to the sites I was able to include based on currently available information.

The collection of samples for this study was necessarily affected by the limits of past research designs and fieldwork as no new excavations were initiated for the sole purpose of this particular study. The majority of contexts in this study were construction fill from structures. The types of structures were varied, from monumental pyramid and rectangular range structures in the core of the site to modest house mound structures in the site peripheries. Samples from each site included as many different contexts as possible to enable the research to address a wider range of issues concerning economic organization.

It should be noted that many more samples were taken from each site than were actually thin sectioned. However, this does not diminish the relevance of the sample size as each sherd sampled was subjected to

macroscopic analysis and formed the preliminary petrofabric groupings. The specifics of this analytical methodology are further outlined in the next chapter, Chapter Four: Analytical Methods.

Site Overviews

In the following site overviews general site descriptions, maps and contexts sampled for each site are discussed in greater detail. To situate each site, I make reference to its location with respect to modern towns and rivers. Where available, an abbreviated site history is sketched with particular focus on the Late Classic period. Notes on surrounding geology and soils are also made providing further context to address the potential for location of pottery raw materials. Since the majority of sites in this study are currently under investigation, much of the information is gleaned from preliminary site reports submitted by researchers to the Department of Archaeology, Belize.

Tables are provided for every site summarizing sample data. Most sites have samples from a number of different internal locations but these contexts are taken together to represent each site in my study. For instance, samples were derived from four different contexts at Cahal Pech and are taken as a whole to represent Cahal Pech. I made this decision because the majority of contexts available for my sampling were construction fill. I deemed construction fill contexts sufficient to indicate that these ceramics were used at the site. A further internal intrasite study based on ceramics from construction fill would be unreliable. I did not undertake this intrasite level of analysis that would require better spatial data indicating use of ceramics at specific loci.

Cahal Pech

Cahal Pech ("The Place of Ticks" in Yucatec and Mopan Maya) is located at the summit of a very steep limestone hill on the west bank of the Macal River, in the outskirts of modern San Ignacio. Satterthwaite (1951), Willey et al. (1965), and Ball and Taschek (1991) have published findings of studies including brief treatment of Cahal Pech among other Belize Valley sites. However, intensive archaeological investigation of the site was not conducted until the late 1980s when Jaime Awe (Awe and Campbell 1988) began a six-year program of research. Awe's investigations revealed early occupation of Cahal Pech dating back to the Early Middle Formative period, 1000 – 850 B.C. Occupation of the site was continuous until the Terminal Late Classic period. During the Late Classic period, Cahal Pech can be classed as a medium-sized centre. The site includes 34 structures dating to the Late Classic, the majority arranged in seven plazas, as well as two ball courts and several uncarved stelae.

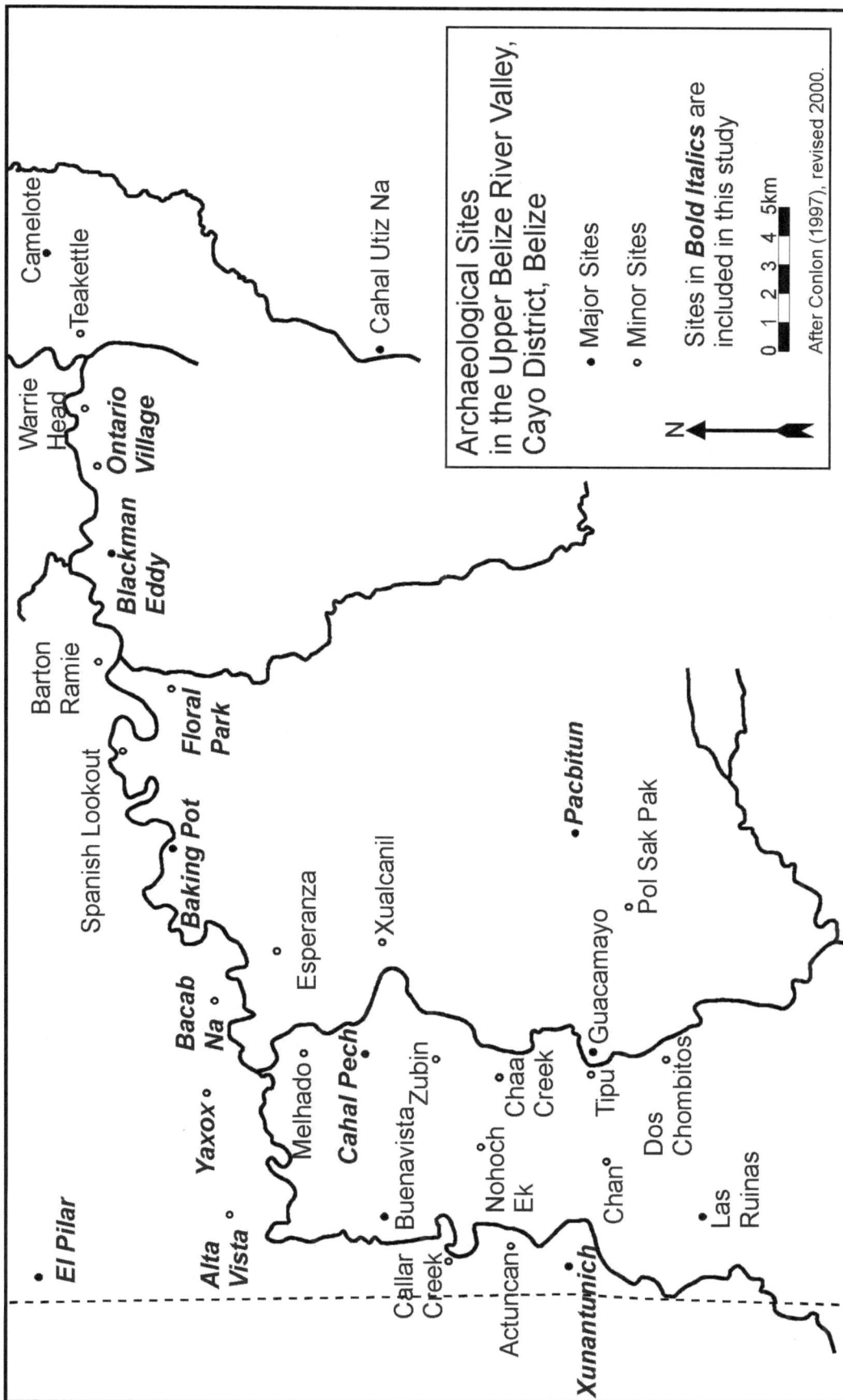

Figure 3.1 Map of Archaeological Sites in the Upper Belize River Valley

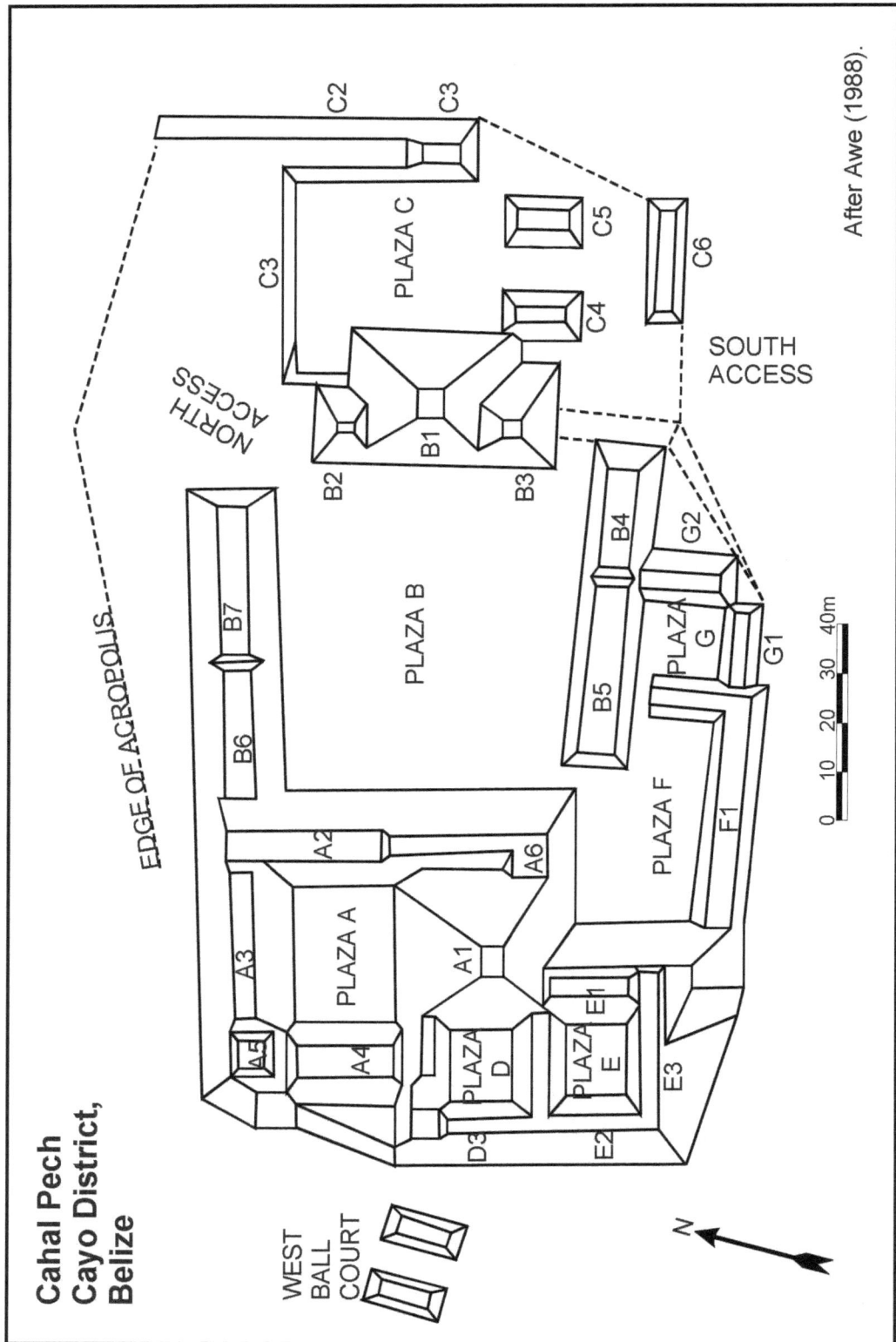

Figure 3.2 Map of Cahal Pech, Cayo District, Belize

Sampled Contexts from Cahal Pech

Samples from Cahal Pech come from a mixture of central and peripheral areas of the site. All samples from each of the locations were from excavated Late Classic contexts of structural fill. A total of 75 sherds were sampled from Cahal Pech. Three main contexts known as Plaza B, Tolok group, K'ik' group and Figueroa group, were selected for sampling at Cahal Pech.

Plaza B is the largest plaza in area (50m by 60m) at Cahal Pech surrounded by monumental pyramidal and range-type (long rectangular structures, generally of lower height than pyramidal building) structures located centrally in the acropolis.

Tolok group, a cluster of 15 structures, is located on the southeastern edge of the site roughly 300m from the Cahal Pech site core. The largest of the structures measures 20m by 12m and is 5m high. Tolok is described as a structure focused settlement cluster (Awe 1992; Powis 1993, 1994).

K'ik' group, found 75m south of the site core, is made up of two rectangular structures the largest of which measures 13m by 5m and is 2m high. Goldsmith (1992, 1993) has characterized K'ik' group as residential in function. Consisting of 12 structures,

Figueroa group is another settlement cluster located on the southwestern periphery of Cahal Pech approximately 300m from the site core.

	Unslipped	Monochrome	Polychrome	Total
# Samples	33	40	2	75
# Thin Sectioned	11	16	1	28

Table 3.1:
Breakdown of Sampled Ceramics from Cahal Pech

Pacbitun

Pacbitun is located in the Cayo District of Belize, approximately ten linear kilometers southeast of the modern town of San Ignacio. First reported and named as a site in 1971 by a past acting commissioner of the Belize Department of Archaeology, Peter Schmidt, the word "Pacbitun" traces its origin to the Maya term "Pacbitunich" which can be translated as "stones set in the earth." In 1980 archaeological work led by Paul Healy started under the organization of the Trent-Cayo Archaeological Project.

The Trent-Cayo Archaeological Project undertook survey, mapping and excavation of the site revealing a medium-sized civic-ceremonial centre. Over forty major structures were identified configured around five plaza areas (Healy 1990, 1992:229). Original occupation of the site appears to have occurred in the Middle Formative period (c. 900 B.C). Pacbitun was abandoned in the Terminal Classic period (c. A.D. 900).

As noted by Healy (1990) and Ritchie (1990), Pacbitun is situated on the boundary between two geographic and ecological zones. The first zone, lowland tropical forest, is typically associated with the valley area. The second zone is the upland pine ridge that covers the Maya Mountains.

Preparatory excavations were conducted in 1984 (Healy 1985). The project's goal was to examine the site and its development in relation to its sustaining area, particularly its terraced environment (Healy 1985:4). Excavations were performed on structures in the core area as well as along two 1100m long transects to the northeast and southeast (Ritchie 1990). The extension of two more mapped and excavated transects from the site core began in 1987 to the northwest and southwest peripheral zones of Pacbitun and have been analysed by Sunahara (1995). Ceramics from Pacbitun included in this study were sampled from transect material from the site periphery and sherds uncovered by excavation of areas in the ceremonial core of the site.

Sampled Contexts from Pacbitun

Three main contexts from within the site of Pacbitun were sampled for ceramics in my study: the Northwest transect, Southwest transect and a cluster of contexts in the site core. The Northwest and Southwest transects mapped a total of 143 structures. The majority (82-89%) of these structures were considered residential (Sunahara 1995:123-124). Only five structures on Southwest and four structures on the Northwest transects were of two construction phases. The majority of structures were of simple one phase cut limestone with earth fill topped with plaster floors. All structures had Late Classic construction as their terminal phase of architecture. Ceramics sampled from the transects came from test pit excavations that were located in the middle of each structure. All samples are considered to be of construction fill contexts.

Four areas in the site core were sampled: (1) the base of Stela 8 on the south western side of structure 13, (2) a burial between structures 1 and 4, (3) base of Stela 4 in the middle of Plaza A and (4) the south ballcourt. It should be noted that though these samples were from burial and rituals contexts, they were not given any special consideration. The following table summarizes sampling information from Pacbitun.

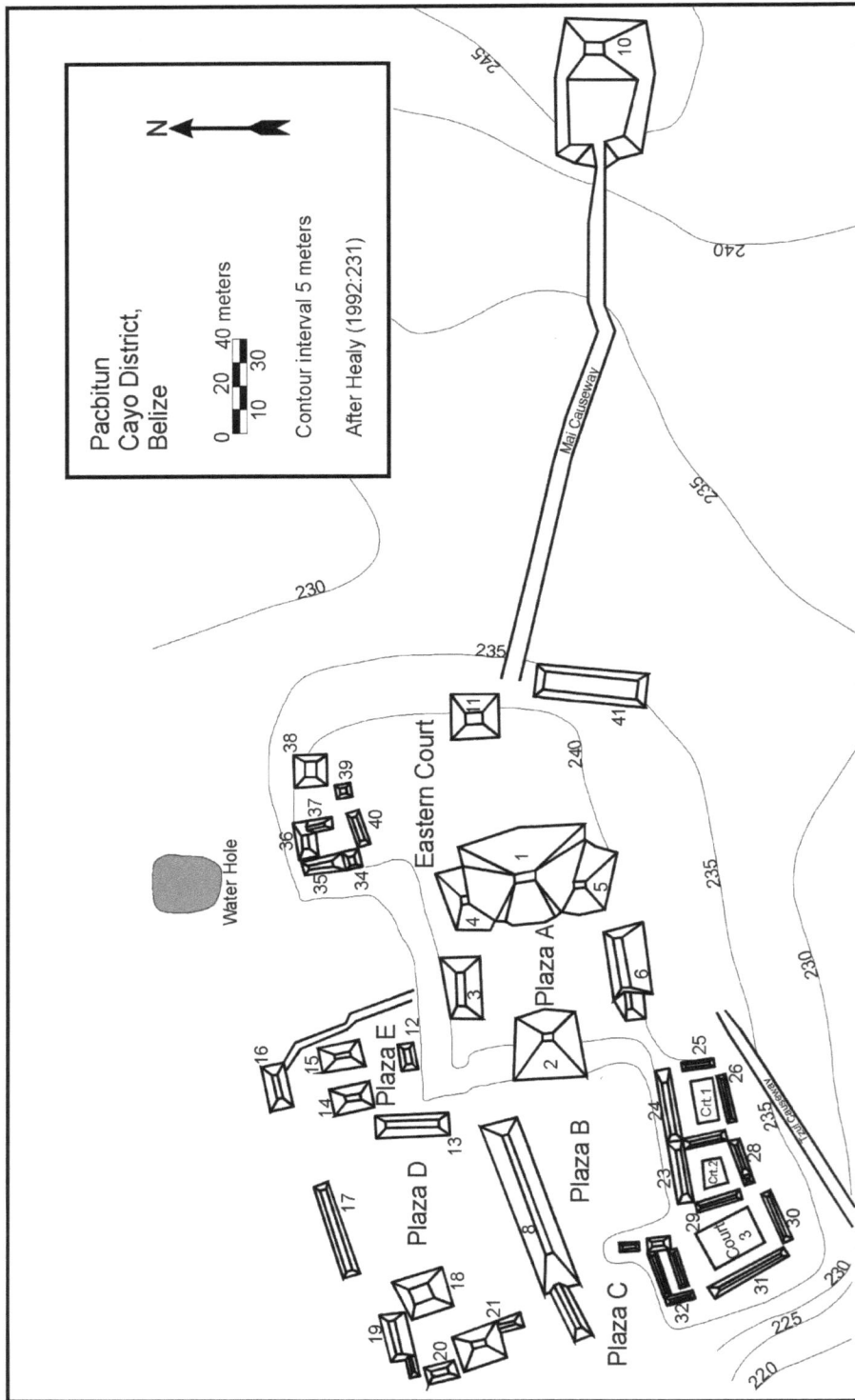

Figure 3.3 Map of Pacbitun, Cayo District, Belize

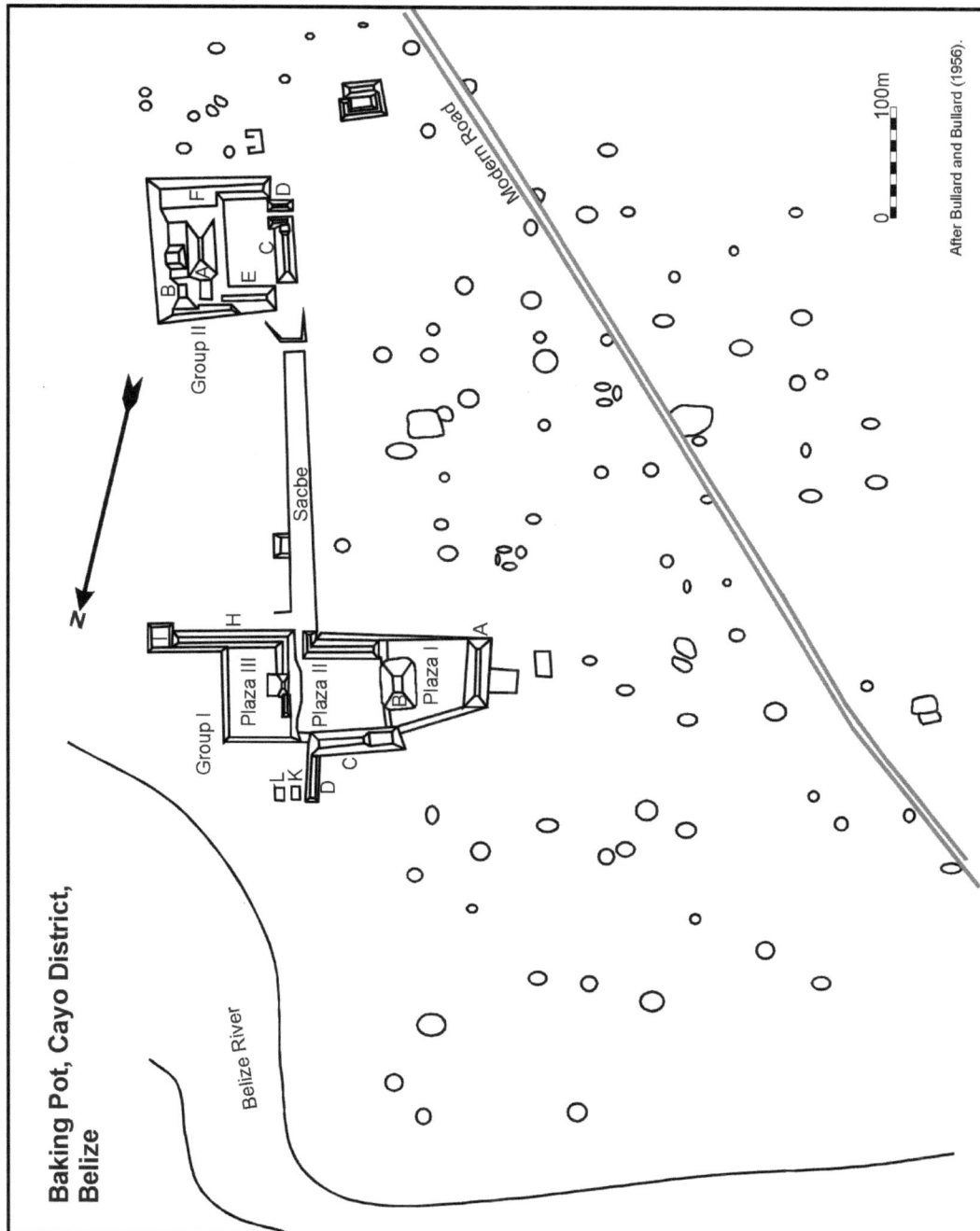

Figure 3.4 Map of Baking Pot, Cayo District, Belize

	Unslipped	Monochrome	Polychrome	Total
# Samples	15	20	3	38
# Thin Sectioned	5	8	2	15

	Unslipped	Monochrome	Polychrome	Total
# Samples	43	67	5	115
# Thin Sectioned	29	31	2	62

Table 3.2:
Breakdown of Sampled Ceramics from Pacbitun

Table 3.3
Breakdown of Ceramic Samples from Baking Pot

Baking Pot

Located five miles northwest of San Ignacio, on the south bank of the Belize River, the site of Baking Pot rests on land that is part of Central Farm, an agricultural station of the Belize government. Presently, the site is predominantly covered by pastureland and low-lying scrub vegetation. Situated close the river, the soil around Baking Pot is fine and alluvial. Baking Pot consists of two major groups of monumental structures joined by a *sacbe*. Full coverage survey conducted by the Belize Valley Archaeological Reconnaissance project mapped a total of 318 structures at Baking Pot small house mounds as well as monumental buildings (Conlon and Ehret 1999:5).

Research at Baking Pot (Willey et al. 1965:308; Bullard and Bullard 1965:9; Aimers 1997:38) has unearthed small traces of occupation in the Late Formative period c. 100 B.C.; however, it is in the Spanish Lookout, Late Classic period when the site appears to have reached its height. The Postclassic is very poorly represented at Baking Pot, represented by a handful of pottery sherds. Due to the ease of accessibility, Baking Pot has been the subject of a number of archaeological investigations starting with Ricketson (1931), A.H. Anderson in 1949, Willey (Willey et al. 1965), and Bullard (1965). The most recent investigations at the site were headed by Awe (1993) and it is from these excavations that ceramic materials were sampled for my study.

Sampled Contexts from Baking Pot

Readily accessible ceramics collections allowed for the sampling of five contexts from Baking Pot: (1) Atalaya group, (2) Structure 193, (3) Plaza II, (4) Structure L, and (5) Bedran group. Atalaya group is a small (the largest of the mounds measured 1.11m in elevation) four mound plazuela group to the south of the site core (Moore 1997:49). Structure 193 is a mound structure located to the south of Group I. Plaza II contexts included sherds from excavations in Structures F and C. Structure L is one of two buildings forming a ballcourt at the northern edge of Group II. Bedran group is four structure plazuela group located 1.8 km to the southwest of the site core. All contexts from Baking Pot are of construction fill. The following table summarizes sample information for the ceramics of Baking Pot.

Xunantunich

One of the western-most sites to be included in my study, Xunantunich ("The Place of the Stone Maiden") is situated on a hilltop overlooking the Mopan River near the modern town of San Jose Succotz. Dominated by a 41m tall structure commonly referred to as "El Castillo," Xunantunich has produced three carved stelae dating to the late 8th and early 9th Century A.D. (Leventhal 1992:3). Ceramic samples for Xunantunich are derived from the latest investigations performed by the Xunantunich Archaeological Project (XAP) headed by Richard Leventhal and Wendy Ashmore during the period of 1991-1997.

Investigators suggest that the occupation of the hilltop began in the Middle Formative. Excavations have uncovered traces of Middle Formative material; however, Middle Formative evidence does not appear to be in original contexts nor has extant architecture dating from this timeframe been found to date. Formative and Late Formative Occupation is found at Xunantunich in the form of a pyramid and Platform group. There is minimal evidence of occupation at Xunantunich during the early Classic period. It is during the Late Classic period and the beginning of the Terminal Classic period that this site appears to flourish. In the terminal Classic proper, evidence of occupation continues at the site but there is evidence that parts of the site were abandoned. Archaeological investigations at Xunantunich have included the excavation and consolidation of structures in the main acropolis, as well as settlement survey investigations (Ashmore 1995, Yaeger 1992) including mapping transects and test pits in house mounds (Ehert 1995).

Sampled Contexts from Xunantunich

Six different contexts from the site core of Xunantunich were available for sampling: (1) Structure A-1, (2) Structure A-5, (3) Structure A-6, (4) Structure A-24, (5) Structure A-25, and (6) Structure D-7. Structure A-1 is a monumental pyramidal structure located in the main Plaza A of the site. Structure A-5 is a platform abutting Structure A-6 to the east. Structure A-6 is a monumental pyramidal building and the most imposing feature at Xunantunich called "El Castillo". Structures A-24 and A-25 are located to over 125m to the west of the main plaza. Structure D-7 is a rectangular building located near the terminus of sacbe I to the east of the Plaza A (Keller 1993:87-99). Contexts from Xunantunich range

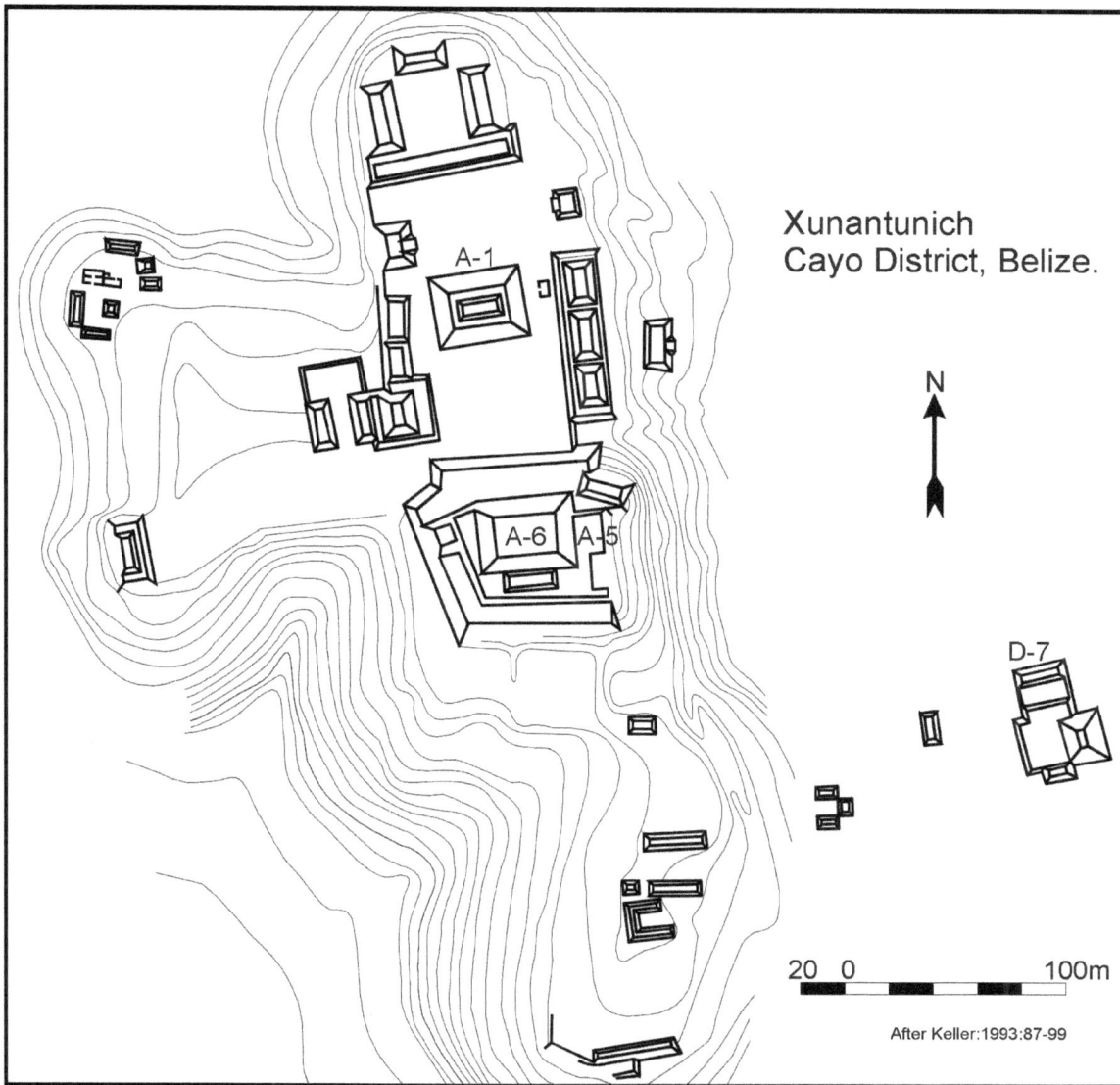

Figure 3.5 Map of Xunantunich, Cayo District, Belize

from construction fill to collapse debris. The following table presents further information on the ceramic samples from Xunantunich.

	Unslipped	Monochrome	Polychrome	Total
# Samples	12	32	8	52
# Thin Sectioned	5	19	4	28

Table 3.4
Breakdown of Ceramic Samples from Xunantunich

Blackman Eddy

Blackman Eddy is located 9.76 km east of the site of Baking Pot. Set on a hilltop the site is situated on the first alluvial terrace south of the Belize River. The Belize Valley Archaeological Project led by James F. Garber from 1990 to 1999 conducted archaeological investigations at Blackman Eddy. Extant architecture consists of twenty-one structures arranged around two plaza areas with the tallest structures reaching 10m in height. One ball court, a partially carved stela and several plain stelae were also recorded.

First occupation of the site occurred during the early Middle Formative Period 650 B.C. – 100 B.C. The site appears to have been abandoned in the Terminal Classic Period to Early Postclassic period c. A.D. 900 (Garber, Brown and Hartman 1998:23). Several smaller plazuela groups surround the ceremonial core of the site and mound clusters.

Sampled Contexts from Blackman Eddy

Two contexts provided samples from Blackman Eddy: (1) Structure A-7 and (2) Structure B-1. Structure A-7 is an L-shaped range structure located on the southwest of the site core; A-7 forms the southern end of the ballcourt (Hartman 1994:21).
Structure B-1 is a monumental pyramidal structure found in the north site core. Samples from B-1 are from

17

operation 15, an eight meter square unit in the southern face of the building that included the final construction phase of the building dating to the Late Classic period (Garber, Reilly and Glassman 1995:6). All contexts from Blackman Eddy are from construction fill.

	Unslipped	Monochrome	Polychrome	Total
# Samples	6	10	1	17
# Thin Sectioned	6	10	1	17

Table 3.5   Breakdown of Ceramic Samples from Blackman Eddy

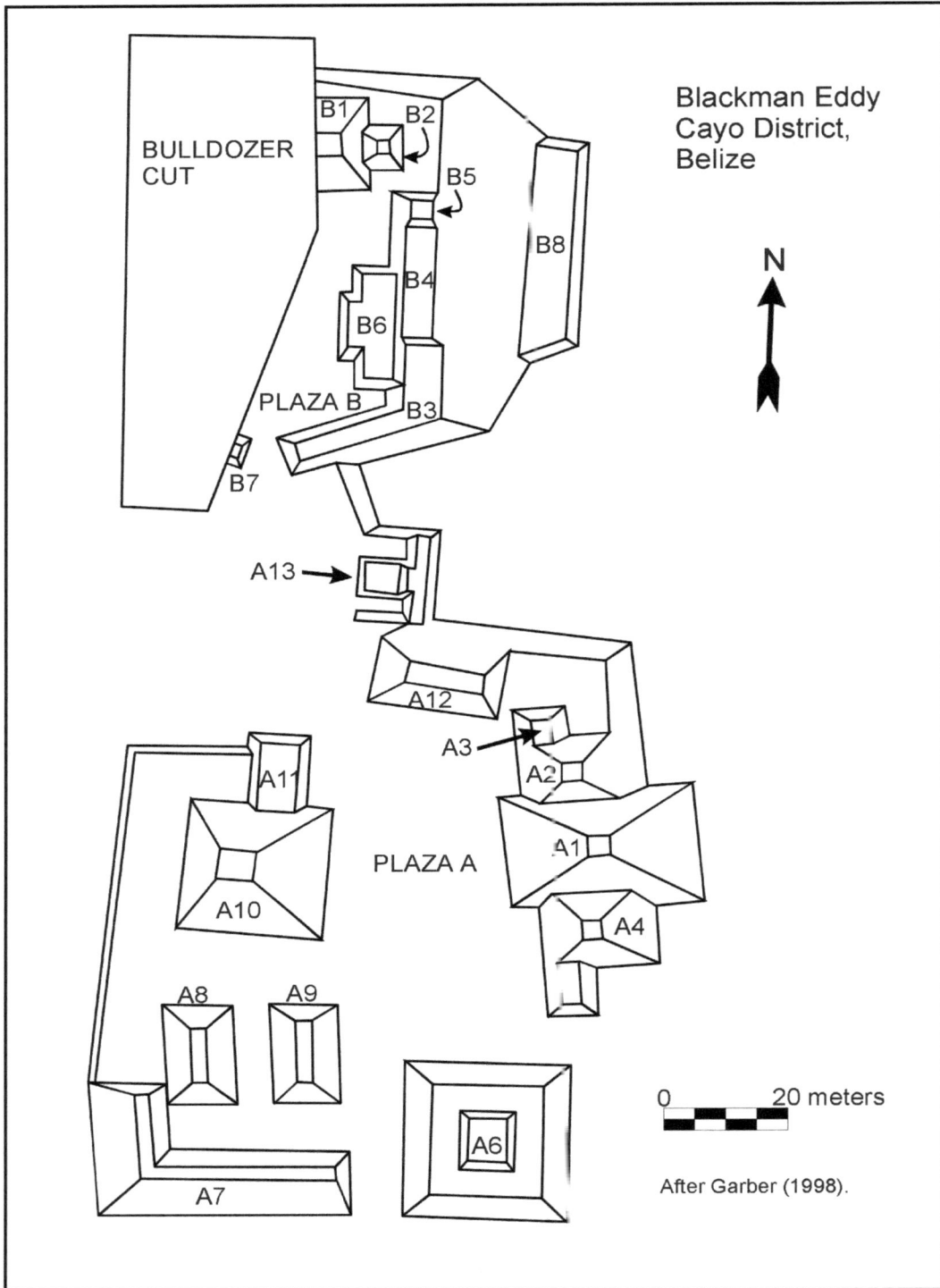

Figure 3.6 Map of Blackman Eddy, Cayo District, Belize

18

Ontario Village

The most easterly site in this study, Ontario Village, is a small ceremonial centre located approximately 3.8 km from the site of Blackman Eddy and 13.3 km west of Belmopan, 300m to the southeast of the Belize River. Investigations by Dr. James F. Garber and the Belize

Valley Archaeological Project in 1993 revealed that Ontario Village was constructed on the floodplain of the valley in the Late Classic Period and abandoned in the Terminal Classic to Early Postclassic Period (Garber et al. 1994:10).

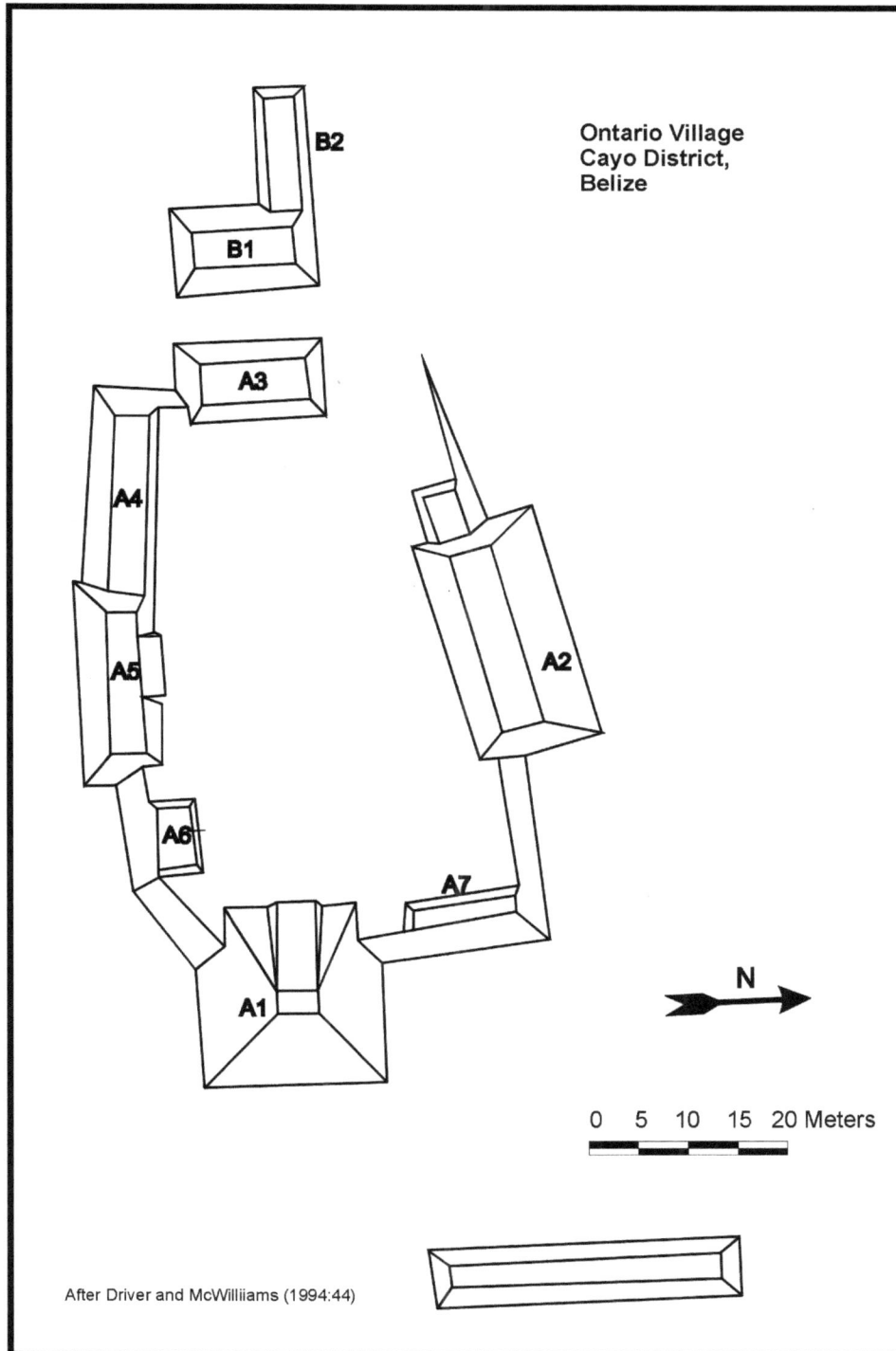

Figure 3.7 Map of Ontario Village, Cayo District, Belize

Described as small ceremonial centre, the site consists of seven structures arranged around one formal public plaza area. An additional two structures at the western edge of the ceremonial core form a small, one construction phase, ball court. One outlying group of two structures, 175m to the south of the main plaza area was also identified and investigated.

Sampled Contexts from Ontario Village

Two structures from Ontario Village provided samples for my study: (1) Structure A-1 and (2) Structure A-5. Measuring approximately 19m square and 6m in height, Structure A-1 is the dominant feature of the site located on the eastern edge of Plaza A. A-1 ceramic samples are from Operation 2a, a 3.5m by 2m excavation on the central axis of the building on its western face (Garber, Glassman, Driver and Weiss 1993:10-11).

Structure A-5 is rectangular building located on the south edge of Plaza A. A-5 measures 22m by 8m and rises 1.8m above the level of the plaza surface (Driver and McWilliams 1995:37). All contexts from Ontario Village sampled for my study are from construction fill. The following table provides an overview of information on Ontario Village samples.

	Unslipped	Monochrome	Polychrome	Total
# Samples	5	11	0	16
# Thin Sectioned	5	11	0	16

Table 3.6
Breakdown of Ceramic Samples from Ontario Village

Floral Park

Floral Park is located approximately 12 km from San Ignacio, south of the Belize River on the valley's alluvial soil. The site itself is a small ceremonial group one kilometer south of the current course of the river. The group consists of two steep mounds, Structure A-1 6.5m high and Structure A-2 5.4m high (Glassman Conlon and Garber 1994:58). Both structures are arranged on a plaza area of irregular crescent shape constructed through the leveling of a limestone bedrock ridge. The two structures are thought to have been pyramidal buildings of ceremonial function (Willey, et al. 1965:310). Smaller mounds are scattered around the main ceremonial grouping and are described by Willey et al. (1965:310) as house mounds, including one cluster of mounds in a formal *plazuela* grouping.

Survey and excavations by the Belize Valley Archaeological Project (Glassman, Conlon and Garber 1995:58-70; Brown et al. 1996:35-62) revealed a large Late Classic, Spanish Lookout occupation at Floral Park. Sherds from these recent investigations were sampled for analysis in my study.

Sampled Contexts from Floral Park

All samples from Floral Park come from Structure A-1, operation 1. Operation 1 consisted of two excavation units, one at the base of the structure and another at its summit. Sherds were more plentiful in the 2m by 3m base unit. Based on the presence of a broken obsidian blade and the high frequency of ceramics all on top of a burnt plaster floor, Glassman, Conlon and Garber (1995:60) suggest that these sherds are the result of a termination ritual. The following table presents sample information on ceramics from Floral Park.

	Unslipped	Monochrome	Polychrome	Total
# Samples	4	8	3	15
# Thin Sectioned	4	8	3	15

Table 3.7
Breakdown of Ceramic Samples from Floral Park

El Pilar

The northernmost site included in this project, El Pilar is located 12 km north of the town of San Ignacio on an interior ridgeland escarpment. Joseph Palacio and Harriet Topsey of the Belize Department of Archaeology first recorded the site in the 1970's. The name El Pilar is Old Spanish for a watering basin. Two local streams, El Pilar Creek and El Manantial (the spring) originate in the vicinity of the site. In 1984, the Belize River Archaeological Settlement Survey (BRASS) project led by Anabel Ford (1990, 1991) began archaeological investigations at El Pilar as part of its mandate. Mapping of the site revealed over 25 plaza areas, situated in an area of approximately 40 hectares spreading over the Belize–Guatemala border. In area, El Pilar is over three times the size of sites such as Baking Pot and Xunantunich. Excavations at El Pilar unearthed an occupation history dating from the Middle Formative (500 B.C.) to Early Postclassic (A.D. 1000). More detailed information regarding the history and apparent significance of El Pilar was not available to me since investigation of the site acropolis is ongoing and publications on these investigations are still in press as of the time of this writing. Three transect surveys were performed as part of the BRASS project, covering three different environmental zones. Ceramic material from El Pilar and its surrounding settlement areas was sampled for this study.

Sampled Contexts for El Pilar

A total of five areas from El Pilar were sampled for my study: (1) Zotz Na 272-005, (2) Alta Vista 272-220, (3) Bacat Na 281-021 and (4) Yaxox 278-026 and (5) Yaxox 278-006. Zotz Na 272-005 is located near number 23 on the El Pilar map (see Figure 3.9) in the core of the site's acropolis. The Zotz Na is actually a room and tunnel area that connects two plaza areas (Ford and Wernecke

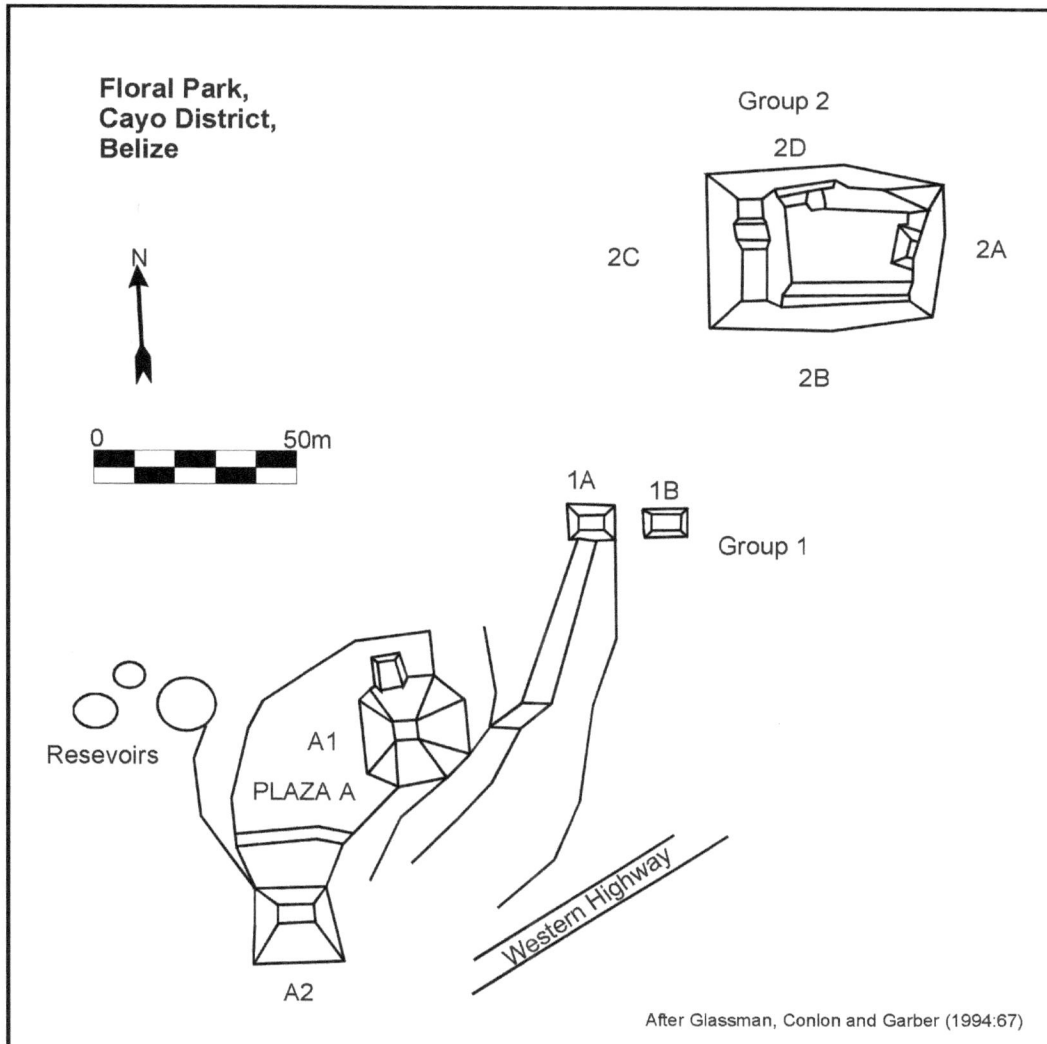

Floral Park,
Cayo District,
Belize

N

0   50m

Group 2

2D

2C   2A

2B

1A   1B

Group 1

Resevoirs

A1

PLAZA A

A2

Western Highway

After Glassman, Conlon and Garber (1994:67)

Figure 3.8 Map of Floral Park, Cayo District, Belize

1996:56-57). The ancient Maya had closed off this area and construction fill here dates to the Late Classic period.

 Three smaller sites found on the settlement transects were also included in this sample since they were determined by Lucero (1994) to be within the surrounding settlement area of El Pilar. Alta Vista 272-220 is a platform structure located 2 km north of the Belize River in a hilly area. Six test pits in this platform structure revealed it was of one Late Classic construction phase.

Yaxox 278-026, is a group of two structures located on the northern bank of the Belize River. These structures were of one construction phase and were determined to be of residential function (Lucero 1994:110-114). Yaxox 278-006 is a small, two construction phase, housemound located in a densely settled flat area.

Lastly, Bacab-Na 281-021 is a medium sized residential site located 0.5 km north of the Belize River (Lucero

1994:115-118). Contexts from each of these settlement areas were designated as from construction fill. The following table provides the breakdown of my ceramic sample from El Pilar.

	Unslipped	Monochrome	Polychrome	Total
# Samples	18	26	0	44
# Thin Sectioned	18	26	0	44

Table 3.8
Breakdown of Ceramic Samples from El Pilar

Sampling Procedure and Summary

Working in field laboratories and storage areas, a sample of Terminal Late Classic material was collected. A concerted effort was made to select samples of sherd material from different *loci* across any given site, such as

21

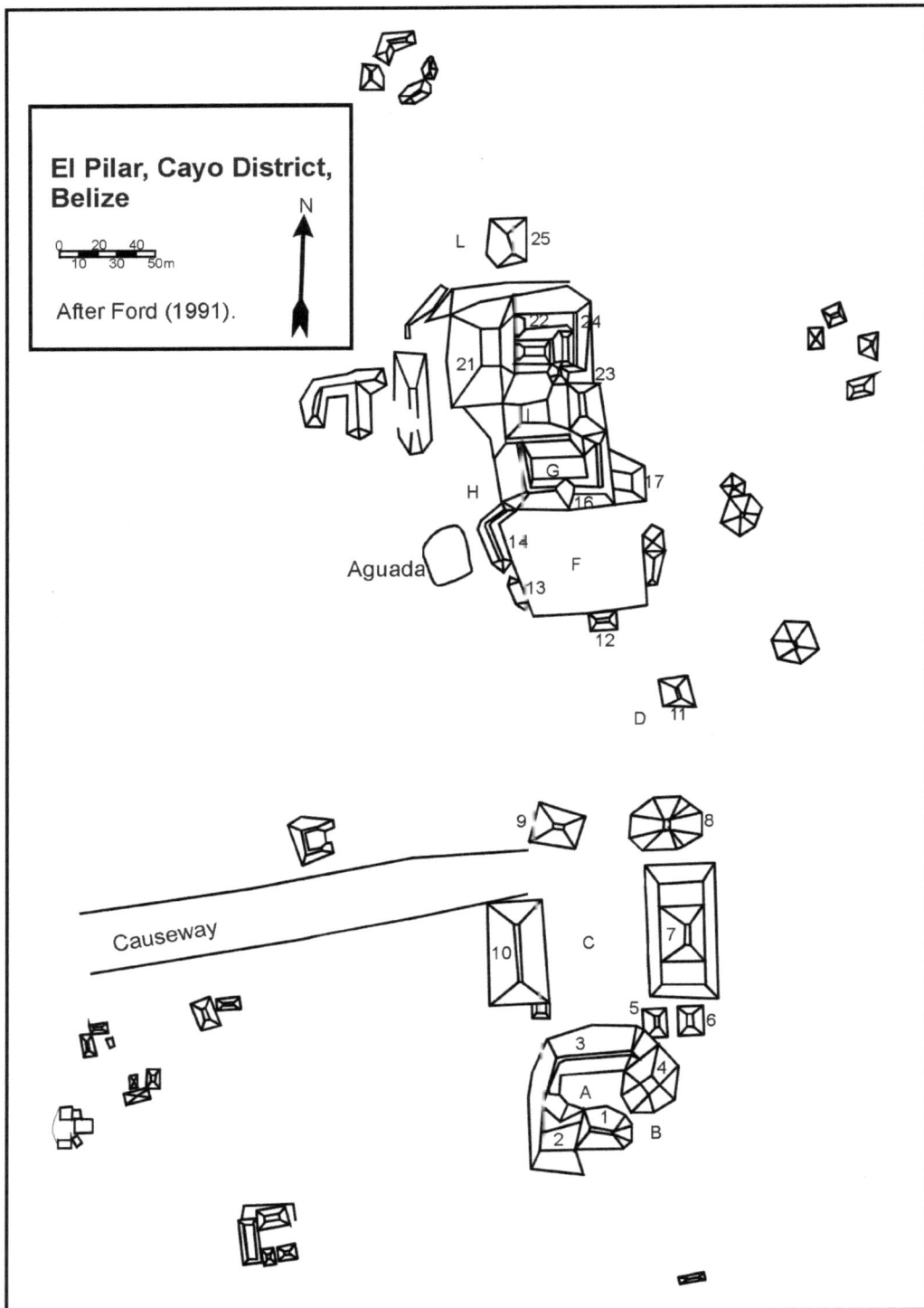

Figure 3.9 Map of El Pilar, Cayo District, Belize

sherds excavated from the site core or acropolis and from the peripheral settlement areas. Some samples were taken from cache, burial and termination deposit contexts; however, I did not select these contexts as a focus for the sampling strategy. The large majority of contexts, as previously detailed in the site summaries, were of construction fill or collapse.

The sampling procedure involved sorting through piles of sherds and breaking off small portions to reveal fresh breaks where inclusions could be better observed and grouped into preliminary petrographically based categories. This was done using a 10x-magnifying lens. As many sherds as accessible were sorted in this manner. The amount of sherds varied greatly from site to site and project to project. For some sites I was limited to studying curated type-collections while at other sites I had greater access to sherds in storage. Additionally, most of the sites in this study were currently under excavation so it was impossible for me to determine the total sampling universe.

After this rough sorting, candidates for thin-section sampling were selected from each group noting the vessel type, and sherd morphology along with the preliminary macroscopic petrographic grouping. Type-variety classifications were also noted where possible but this was not a determining factor in the petrographic sampling.

As a secondary criterion, the selection included slipped types of different colours, unslipped vessels and vessels of different formal and functional attributes. A range of vessel forms including dishes, bowls, ollas, when identifiable was selected; however, due to the fill contexts of most of the available material, great emphasis was not placed on these selection criteria.

Table 3.9 provides an overview of all the 372 sherds that I sampled from the eight sites in my study, with divisions indicating amounts for unslipped, monochrome and polychrome sherds.

During the sampling and analysis information was collected and recorded on a data collection form to ensure uniformity of the data set. Please refer to Appendix B for a copy of the data collection form used. This data collection form was used during sampling and initial macroscopic examination as well as during the actual analysis of thin sections. Both ceramic and raw materials were subjected to the same procedures. A more detailed account of the purpose for and execution of my raw materials sampling program is presented in the next chapter on analytical methods.

Site Name	Unslipped	Monochrome	Polychrome	Total
Cahal Pech	33	40	2	75
Pacbitun	15	20	3	38
Baking Pot	43	67	5	115
Xunantunich	12	32	8	52
Blackman Eddy	6	10	1	17
Ontario Village	5	11	0	16
Floral Park	4	8	3	15
El Pilar	18	26	0	44
Total	136	214	22	372

Table 3.9 Total Sample Size for all Sites

Site Name	Unslipped	Monochrome	Polychrome	Total
Cahal Pech	11	16	1	28
Pacbitun	5	8	2	15
Baking Pot	29	31	2	62
Xunantunich	5	19	4	28
Blackman Eddy	6	10	1	17
Ontario Village	5	11	0	16
Floral Park	4	8	3	15
El Pilar	18	26	0	44
Total	83	129	13	225

Table 3.10 Total Samples Thin Sectioned for all Sites

Description of Field Research

In 1995, two weeks were spent in Belize to determine the potential for a study involving petrographic analysis of ceramics to address the issue of ceramic economy from the regional perspective of the Belize River Valley. After canvassing researchers in the field and an examination of excavated ceramic materials, it was determined that a study encompassing the western Belize River Valley region would be suitable for the aims of my research.

Directors of various archaeological projects in the Belize Valley region were asked to contribute by providing access to excavated collections. Most researchers welcomed the prospect of sampling and petrographic analysis of their pottery as a complement to the standard ceramic typological studies already underway as part of their own investigations. Over 1996 and 1997 sampling from the collections of the eight sites was performed.

As part of the 1997 field season, a raw materials sourcing program was implemented to refine knowledge of local geology and provide greater resolution than that offered by geological maps of the region. The ceramic and raw materials samples were then thin sectioned at the Ceramic Petrology Laboratory, Royal Ontario Museum. Petrological analyses and characterization was done at the same facility on a polarizing petrographic microscope. Detailed accounts of these procedures are provided in the next chapter.

4

Analytical Methods

Introduction: Ceramic Petrology

In this chapter, I outline my methods of analysis within the context of a discussion of the significance of ceramic petrology to archaeology. I draw case studies from geographically diverse areas to serve as examples of different approaches to the archaeological application of ceramic petrology. Initially, I present a brief definition of ceramic petrology as a discipline that lies at the intersection of geology and mineralogy. Its relevance to archaeology is then articulated by the discussions of the analytical techniques used. Finally, I discuss the rationale for methods employed in my research and present details of sample preparation and the raw materials sourcing I performed.

The archaeological application of ceramic petrology is an excellent example of the use of multiple approaches to address questions of past human behaviour. A comprehensive historical overview of the uses of petrology and petrographic thin sectioning in the analysis of archaeological pottery is not possible here (see Williams 1983). However, it should be mentioned that Peacock (1969, 1982) used petrographic techniques to examine the composition of Neolithic pottery recovered from sites in Cornwall in southern England and of later Roman-era ceramic material. Closer to home, Sheppard (1939) has examined materials from the Maya site of San Jose. These researchers were pioneers in the use of ceramic petrology and petrography in archaeology. Since these initial efforts, petrological techniques in archaeological settings has seen a steady increase over time (Angelini 1998; Freestone 1995; Freestone, Johns and Potter 1980; Iceland 1999; Jones 1986; Mason 1994).

Pottery containing rock and mineral inclusions can be examined using the analytical techniques of optical mineralogy. These techniques involve thin sectioning individual ceramic sherds under a polarizing microscope. In this way the mineral composition of a ceramic fabric is defined. Non-plastic inclusions are the objects of analyses. Temper is a term often used to refer to non-plastic inclusions in pottery. It must be noted following Rice (1987c:408-411) that the term "temper" refers specifically to materials purposefully added to the clay by the potter in the production process. The term "non-plastic inclusions" is used to refer to both materials naturally occurring in clay deposits, as well as purposefully added rocks and minerals.

Clay particles are too fine, and are destroyed in the firing process, to be examined with the conventional petrographic microscope. Ceramic bodies containing little to no aplastic inclusions, or very fine-grained inclusions less than 0.03mm, are not appropriate candidates for petrological analysis through thin sectioning and the use of a microscope (Peacock 1970:381). Fortunately, most Maya ceramic material is well suited to petrographic analysis.

Provenance

Thin sectioning and viewing the fabric beneath a polarizing light microscope can identify most non-plastic inclusions in the clay mineralogically. Mineralogical identifications are attributes that form part of a petrofabric definition. Groupings of similar definitions form the basis for the characterization of petrofabric groups. A typology based on ceramic petrological attributes can be compiled. This mineralogical identification is particularly useful in situations where inclusions from unique, or exotic, sources occur (Williams 1983:323). In certain specific cases, the presence of a particular mineral inclusion can be traced back to its temper source. In order to trace provenance, reliable geological maps of the region studied and surrounding areas need to be available. It is also advisable that supplemental information on local geology be augmented by a pottery raw materials resource survey. The sourcing of local materials helps greatly in the recognition of local versus non-local mineral components.

This methodology for distinguishing between locally produced pottery and imported ceramics has been applied in numerous studies. Mason and Cooper (1999) have examined early Transcaucasian pottery from Godin Tepe in Iran dating to the third millennium B.C. One of their significant findings was that a large quantity of the pottery assemblage from the site at that time contained materials that were not derived from the local region (Mason and Cooper 1999:29). Observing that, (1) local sources of raw materials could have easily sufficed to make the pottery in question but were not used, (2) there was a significant technological innovation in the use of grog temper, and (3) the pottery was distinct stylistically, Mason and Cooper (1999:29-30) suggest that this ceramic evidence indicates the presence of a new population at Godin Tepe. They characterize this new population as practicing a transhumant lifestyle partly based on nomadic pastorialism. The movement of people is equated with the movement of pots and also helps to explain the non-local petrological composition found in the pottery. Their assertion is further supported by faunal evidence of sheep and goat remains as well as recorded changes in the disposition of settlement and architectural features.

Using the same principle of petrological provenance, Morris' (1991:285) examination of pottery from the late Bronze Age-early Iron Age settlement at Potterne in Wiltshire, England, has demonstrated a shift in local to non-local pottery over time. Pottery from earlier periods was of local materials and manufacture. Pottery from Potterne's later periods was characterized by the introduction of ceramics made at another site, with a distinctive petrological make-up, found 15 km away.

Provenance Issues

It is important for archaeologists to note that if successful this type of provenance study will only trace the ceramic temper to its geological point of origin. The geological origin of the ceramic temper does not necessarily directly equate to the locus of ceramic production. Limits to this approach are imposed by the extent and resolution of geological studies and surveys available for the regions under consideration. It is evident that mineralogical and geological analysis alone is not adequate to address issues concerned with the production and use of the pottery by past peoples. Wardle (1992:15) observes that factors such as trade in the actual tempering material can seriously affect the relevance of this conventional interpretive method for archaeological samples.

An example of this situation has been outlined by Simmons and Brem (1979) for volcanic ash tempered pottery from the Yucatan region of the Lowland Maya sub-area. Simmons and Brem (1979:81-83) were able to identify volcanic ash as a component of temper in ceramics from Dzibilchaltun, state of Yucatan, Mexico. This identification was by no means the solution to a problem, but the root of many more questions to be asked. The explanation of how volcanic ash ended up in ceramics produced in a non-volcanic, limestone geological environment was primary among the new research questions posed by the authors. After testing ash samples from various sources in the Maya sub-area it was postulated that volcanic ash from highland Guatemala or El Salvador was traded into the Yucatan, possibly in exchange for salt (Simmons and Brem 1979:79). The identification of volcanic ash and subsequent geological surveys has required that archaeologists look to alternative models to describe the trade and economics of pottery in the northern Maya Lowlands. Volcanic ash was also found in samples included in my study and I provide an alternative to Simmons and Brem's stance in chapter six.

Provenance, another approach

The collection of kiln wasters, kiln furniture such as trivets, and the excavation of actual pottery production areas addresses some of the concerns relating to the significance of petrographically established provenance illustrated in the previous example from the Maya area. The definition of various production centres by excavation of production loci using ceramics from specific kiln sites facilitates the definition of petrofabrics characteristic of individual centres.

This approach was used by Mason and Keall (1988) in their examination of medieval Islamic ceramics from Zabid, Yemen. Goals of their study focused on the establishment of a ceramic typology that included the determination of which ceramics were imported or local in origin. The typology established by Mason and Keall's research formed the basis for ceramic chronology in a relatively unexplored archaeological region of the world. More detailed questions regarding the ability of petrography to distinguish between two production centres, and the ability to identify materials imported into the Near East from elsewhere, were posed for future study.

The paucity of located production sites prevents the usage of this particular approach for archaeologists working in the Maya area and in my current research; yet, its potential should not be neglected. The significance of provenance information generated by the approach of Mason and Keall adds incentive for the discovery of such loci.

Textural Analysis

In addition to the mineralogical identification of temper material, inclusions can be subjected to textural analysis. Textural analysis involves the characterization of a ceramic fabric by counting inclusions, as well as describing their shape and spatial orientation. This type of analysis can be performed on both thin sectioned material as well as pottery that is cut to expose one section (thick); however, it is usually recommended that textural studies be done on thin sectioned ceramics for sake of greater objectivity and clarity (Orton, Tyers and Vince 1993:141). Thin sections allow for greater ease when viewing textural attributes. Textural analysis can be done to characterize pottery where there is difficulty in identifying inclusions mineralogically or where a significant percentage of the assemblage presents fabrics that are essentially similar in mineralogical composition. Pottery fabrics are described on the basis of number, shape, size, and distribution of the non-plastic inclusions observed. These data are presented as grain size distributions in graphical or written format in petrological reports. Different fabric groupings are defined on differences in textual attributes. This method has allowed studies to differentiate between ceramics of similar conventional stylistic and formal types and mineralogical composition.

By combining textural and mineralogical forms of thin section analysis with x-ray diffraction, Hays and Hassan (1974) have been better able to define cultural interactions between groups sharing similar pottery styles in the Neolithic period of northern Sudan. It should be noted that Hays and Hassan found petrological analysis to be better able to distinguish different sherds than the x-ray diffraction analysis of the clay. "It can be concluded that the sherds are much less differentiated in terms of their clay mineralogy [x-ray diffraction] than they are on the basis of their petrography" (Hays and Hassan 1974:78).

Freestone observes certain weaknesses in textural analysis:

> The basic assumption behind many of these studies is that the grain size distribution of the products of a single centre varies within a narrow range which differs from examples of the same ware produced elsewhere. In a significant proportion of cases this assumption does not hold (Freestone 1991:405).

Freestone (1991:405) cites the intentional choice of temper grades by potters as a deranging factor in textural analysis. Certainly, potters would select fine grained or coarse grained temper depending on the intended function of a vessel. Fluctuations and gradations in the quality of the temper source itself are also another source of error in textural studies.

Textural analysis can also be combined with the mineral identification of inclusions as has been done by Mason (1991:203), and Mason and Keall (1988:457). Using the full variety of petrographic attributes in tandem with archaeological data logically produces the most significant results.

Methodological Issues

A prevalent caveat offered up with the results of petrographic thin section studies is the issue of relevant sample size. Whatever suggestions made, or trends observed, researchers warn, are to be moderated by this limitation. This valid issue is one that plagues archaeology in general and archaeometric studies are certainly not exempt. The approach outlined by Mason (1994:10) used in this study allows for larger sample sizes to be considered. In the approach used here, hundreds of samples were processed in a preliminary macroscopic survey. Each petrographic sample is in fact treated as representative of a larger grouping. Variations in ceramics missed in the macroscopic surveys are ideally observed during microscopic analyses and groupings are modified and new groups may be added. Microscopic analysis not only enables the identification of a petrofabric's mineral components, but also allows for the description of textural attributes that are key elements in a petrofabric definition. Sampling strateg ies characteristic of other archaeometric methods under the same logistical restraints may only include a handful of samples. Despite this edge, petrographic thin section studies need to be as

explicit about their sampling methodology as they are about the presentation of the mineralogical components of the ceramics they analyse.

All ceramic material used in this study is from provenanced archaeological contexts as have been described in the previous chapter. Many of the samples included were already sorted according to the frequently used Type-Variety classification technique. The particular typology used in the Belize Valley is that of James C. Gifford (1976) *Prehistoric Pottery Analysis and the Ceramics of Barton Ramie in the Belize Valley*. As mentioned briefly above, in each case, sampling began with an initial sorting process where tentative ceramic fabric groups were formed for each site. These groupings were defined according to macroscopic observations made on freshly broken sections of pottery sherds. In this manner, every sherd made available for the study was scrutinized. It was from these preliminary groupings that samples for actual thin sectioning were extracted. Samples to be thin sectioned from preliminary groupings were selected to represent the broadest possible range of petrofabric attributes within the grouping. Some attempt was also made to include samples from a variety of vessels forms, where vessel forms could be determined, that were found within the grouping.

Comments on Archaeometry

In performing this survey of the literature on ceramic petrography, some important issues were recognized. Most significant was the often weak level of integration between archaeometric analyses and the archaeological and anthropological questions toward which they are directed. With the exception of a few articles it was hard to establish exactly what research questions were being asked of the ceramic material and why the petrographic method of investigation was used. The context of the petrographic research needs to be better articulated within a broader anthropological matrix and effectively communicated. Goals of investigations need to be plainly apparent. As DeAtley and Bishop (1991:365-366) mention, the major issue of communication is significant for the petrological study of ceramics as well as the host of other scientific techniques of investigation employed by archaeology.

Archaeometric studies need to outline the over-arching theoretical basis of their research and how their results contribute to an understanding of a particular economic, social or anthropological phenomenon. The point of articulation between the research question, theory and archaeometry needs to be thoroughly explored by investigators. Results of analyses need to be interpreted in a clearly described contextual framework that includes an explanation of what archaeological and anthropological questions are being addressed. Doing so will prevent the marginalization of these considerable efforts.

Having contextually framed my research questions and how they can be addressed by petrographic analyses in previous chapters, in the following two sections, I discuss the details of how petrographic analysis was done in my study. I also explain how and why raw materials sourcing was implemented.

Petrographic Analysis in this Study

The following discussion outlines the physical preparation of thin section specimens. I end this section with a listing of the mineral inclusions that were identified in my study.

Jones (1996:85) found that in most cases a sample of 1cm by 0.5cm was sufficient for analysis. In most cases a sample of roughly 3cm by 2cm was taken for this study. Size of the sample varied according to the friability of specimen as well as the size of the inclusions. The larger the inclusions, larger was the size of the sample taken for thin sectioning.

The specimens were exported back to Canada with permission from the Belize Department of Archaeology to undergo thin sectioning at the facilities of the Royal Ontario Museum Ceramic Petrology Laboratory. Figure 4.1 represents the thin sectioning process. There, the specimens were submerged in a liquid epoxy matrix, subjected to two 15 minute intervals in a vacuum chamber and set to cure overnight on a hotplate. This process impregnated the pores of the fabric to limit friability during thin sectioning ensuring that all inclusions would be represented in the final thin section.

Once cured the specimens were ground down on one face with a lapidary grinder and affixed to a glass slide with more epoxy. Lastly, the rest of the ceramic on the slide was ground away in a petrographic sectioning machine leaving a thin section of ceramic. The thin section was then covered with a glass slip and viewed beneath a polarizing light microscope.

The primary categories of mineral inclusions that were observed in this study were:

- Calcite (micritic & crystalline)
- Quartz
- Plagioclase (feldspar)
- Microcline (feldspar)
- Orthoclase (feldspar)
- Volcanic ash/glass
- Shell
- Biotite and Muscovite (micas)
- Chert
- Magnetite (opaques)
- Hematite (opaques).

An asset of petrographic method, despite being classified as "destructive", is that a slide collection of thin sections has been compiled. This has left a reference collection that can be used for future comparison.

Raw Materials Sourcing

Samples of sands, soils and some clay were collected as part of this study and conducted in the 1997 field season. This was done to supplement information provided by geological maps I obtained of the region.

The sampling strategy was primarily guided by the objective to seek materials that might have been accessible and used by the Late Classic Maya in pottery production. As a result, each of the locales from which samples were gathered is currently in proximity to, if not actually at, archaeological sites included in my study. This strategy is also supported by ethnoarchaeological work done by Arnold (1985:36) that suggests ancient potters preferred to use raw materials sources that were available nearby. According to Arnold (1985:50), 33% of potters he studied sourced their pottery raw materials within 1 km and 84% of potters found their supplies within a 7 km radius of their production areas.

Raw materials samples were thoroughly dried at the lab in Belize and exported to Canada where I prepared them into thin sections for petrological analysis. The results of these analyses revealed the mineralogical composition and granulometry of the samples in much the same way as the analyses of the pottery thin sections. In this manner, a data set comparable to the pottery thin sections was made. By comparing the mineral composition of raw materials sections and pottery sections, the raw materials samples aided me in the definition of what ceramic petrofabrics might be considered locally derived and produced. Another specific objective was to demonstrate the presence or the absence of volcanic ash in locally available raw materials.

Raw materials were sourced along riverbeds and banks. Banks along sections of the Mopan, Macal and Belize Rivers were surveyed where access could be gain via road and/or navigation by canoe. Figure 4.2 details riverine areas covered in these sampling expeditions. Stops were made at eroding clay outcrops and where sand deposits were encountered along the rivers' banks.

A series of three canoe expeditions covered the river systems. The first transversed Chaa Creek to San Ignacio on the Macal River. Figure 4.3 shows an eroded area sampled at the confluence of the Macal and Mopan Rivers just outside of San Ignacio (sample MA10 was taken here). Figure 4.4 shows a bank on the Macal River where a deposit of sand was sampled (sample MA5 was taken here).

PETROGRAPHIC ANALYSIS: HOW IT WORKS

Different production centres will have different types of inclusions in the pottery body.
So when we find pottery with the same range of inclusions we know it came from that production centre.

CLAY MATRIX

VOLCANIC ROCK

FELDSPAR

QUARTZ

BIOTITE

Under the microscope, the various rocks and minerals that are in the body may be identified.

A small piece has been cut out of this broken pot.

The piece is then ground very flat on one side and is then glued to a glass slide.

The piece of pottery is ground down until it is only 0.03mm thick.

It is now so thin, you can see through it. This is called a *thin-section*.

The thin-section is then put in a polarising microscope.

Cross-polarized light, all light blocked unless diffracted by crystals

POLARISER

Light diffracted by crystals in sample

SAMPLE

Plane-polarised light vibrates in one direction

POLARISER

Ordinary light - vibrates in all directions

LIGHT

DIAGRAM showing methodology of petrographic analysis. Once the thin-section is made it is viewed through a polarising microscope, which has two polarising filters oriented at right-angles to each other, thereby blocking out any light. However, a sample containing minerals may diffract the light, so that they are visible in cross-polarized light. The degree of diffraction is a key characteristic enabling identification of the crystals.

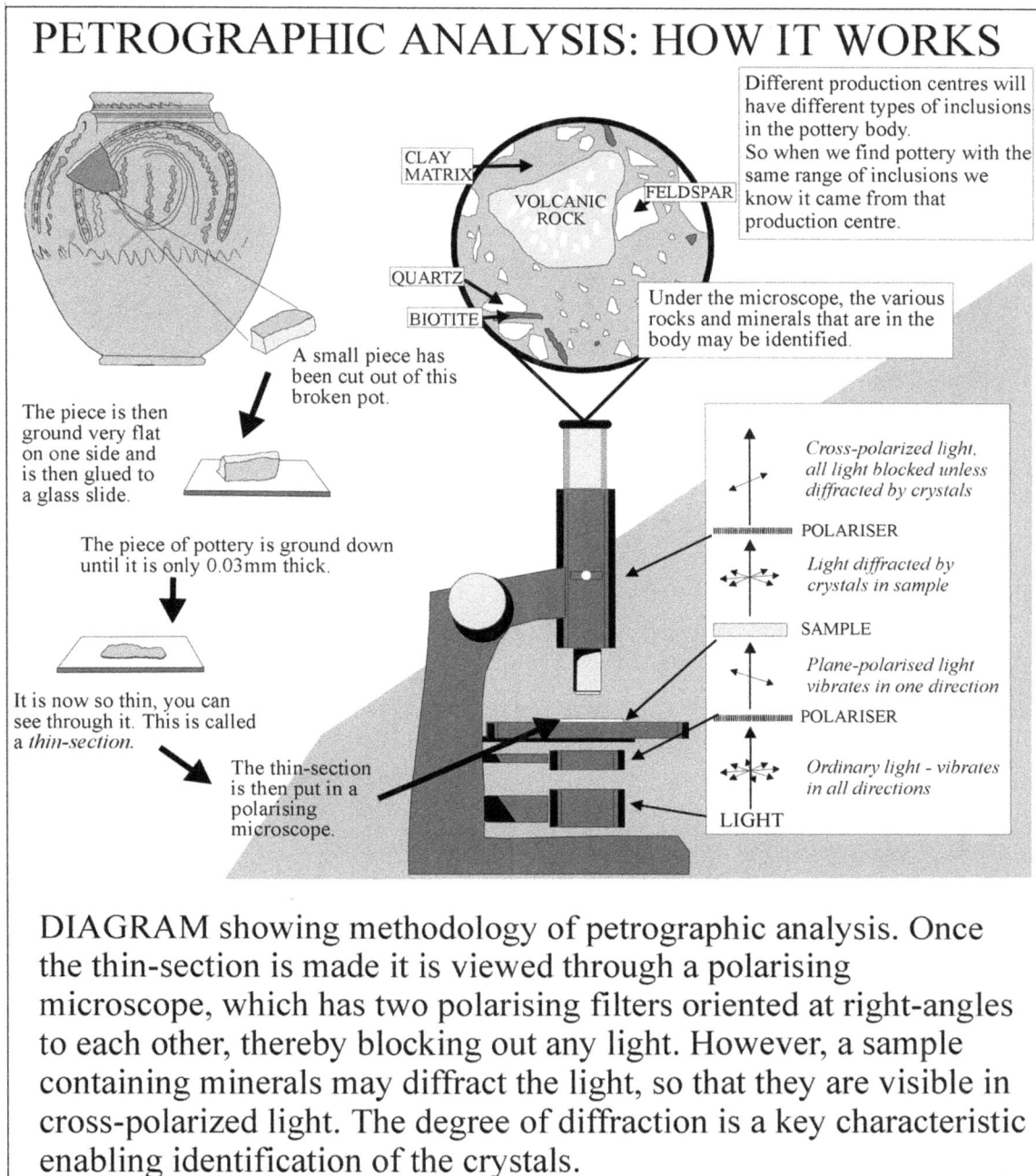

Figure 4.1 Flowchart of Steps in Petrographic Analysis, from Mason (1994)

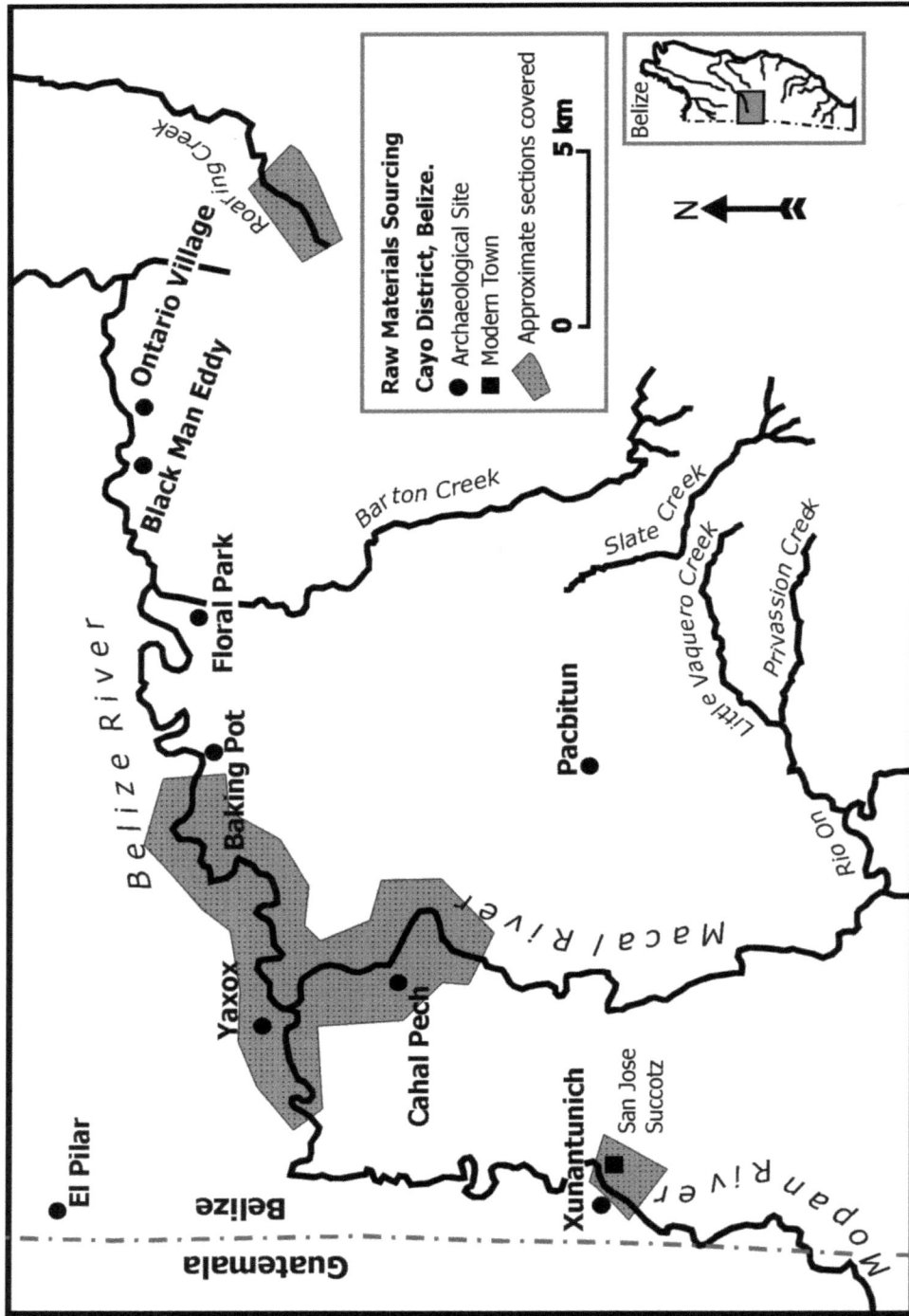

Figure 4.2 Map of Riverine Areas Covered in Raw Materials Sampling.

Figure 4.3 View of "Branchmouth" Confluence of Macal and Mopan Rivers.

Figure 4.4 Bank of the Macal River and Sand Deposit

Figure 4.5 Creek emptying into the Belize River, Western bank.

The second covered Bullet Tree Falls to San Ignacio on the Mopan River. The third ran from San Ignacio to Baking Pot on the Belize River. This covered sections of the two tributaries (Macal and Mopan Rivers) of the Belize River as well as a portion of the Belize River proper. Figure 4.5 shows a sampled location where clay samples were taken at the mouth of a small creek emptying into the Belize River (samples BZ3 and BZ4 were taken here).

Further sourcing along the Belize River east of Baking Pot would also have been desirable; unfortunately, budgetary and time constraints did not make this possible. While the logistical difficulties of sampling of clay sources over the large expanse of the Belize River Valley were a limiting factor in the choice of sample locations, I was also concerned with selecting zones that would have been accessible to prehispanic people and their settlements.

The Roaring Creek River is another tributary of the Belize River joining the river just west of Belmopan, having its source in the Mountain Pine Ridge. Creeks, streambeds, and cave systems along the Roaring Creek River provided further samples. Numerous caves along the Roaring Creek River have been reconnoitered by the Western Belize Region Cave Project (Awe, Helmke and Griffith 1997). The opportunity presented itself to take samples from inside these caves; as a result, samples taken from Actun Tunichil Muknal, Actun Uayazaba Kab, and Actun Yaxteel Ahau (also known as Pancho Carranza Cave) have been added to the raw materials collection. Graham et al (1980) have reported archaeological evidence for clay extraction from inside Footprint Cave in a different cave system, the Caves Branch system, to the south. The possibility that pottery raw materials such as clay might have been sourced in caves warranted the inclusion of the few caves accessible to me during my fieldwork stay.

Samples were also collected in St. Herman's Cave part of the Caves Branch River and cave system that flows into the Sibun River. Caves Branch is a separate river system draining the Sibun Gorge located to the east the Mountain Pine Ridge. The Sibun River empties into the Caribbean Sea to the south of the Belize River. St. Herman's Cave is outside the immediate study area of the Belize River Valley but samples were nonetheless included since the opportunity arose to obtain sand from the cave. Additionally, though not extensively studied by archaeologists (no formal publications were available to me at the time of my research), St. Herman's Cave is know as a major location of Late Classic activity and is found to contain pottery and lithic artifacts.

Table 4.1 is a complete listing of all raw materials samples taken with sample number, location and context. In total 45 samples were taken during the raw materials sourcing program.

#	Location, ie: River/Cave	Context
AT1	Cave, Actun Tunichil Muknal	Wall near Datum 14, Grid squares II 191-JJ 191
AT2	Cave, Actun Tunichil Muknal	SE of Datum 28, Olla altar, behind
AT3	Cave, Actun Tunichil Muknal	SE of Datum 27, Grid:LL 177 flowstone dam
AT4	Cave, Actun Tunichil Muknal	Sandbar before stela chamber
AT5	Cave, Actun Tunichil Muknal	Breakdown area before crystal skeleton chamber
AT6	Cave, Actun Tunichil Muknal	Breakdown area before crystal skeleton chamber
UK1	Cave, Actun Uayazaba Kab	Front of cave before escarpment exposed by path
UK2	Cave, Actun Uayazaba Kab	Entrance section, near Datum 33, flowstone dam
UK3	Cave, Actun Uayazaba Kab	Zuhuy Ha, pool chamber, Datums 55 56
UK4	Cave, Actun Uayazaba Kab	Flowstone beyond Zuhuy Ha pool area
YA1	Cave, Yaxteel Ahau	Inside passage, flowing water
SH1	Cave, St. Herman's Cave	Collected by Peter Zubrozycki
SH2	Cave, St. Herman's Cave	Underground river area
BP1	Baking Pot, Matrix sample	Atalaya, Str.1 Unit3 Level3, housemound
BP2	Baking Pot, Matrix sample	Str193 Unit16 Level3 Lot43, N of wall5, S of wall5
BP3	Baking Pot, Matrix sample	Str.193 Unit 16 Level 3 Lot 43, N of wall 1
LB1	Laughing Bird Caye, beach	Laughing Bird Caye, Placentia, beach
MA1	River Bank, Macal	Mile 3
MA2	River Bank, Macal	Mile 3.5, Cristo Rey North Bank
MA3	River Bank, Macal	Mile 3.5 Cristo Rey
MA4	River Bank, Macal	South Bank, 4 miles from bridge
MA5	River Bank, Macal	Ixchel/Chaa Creek area
MA6	River Bank, Macal	East Bank, North of Bridge
MA7	River Bank, Macal	East Bank North of Bridge, same locus as above
MA8	River Bank, Macal	NE Bank
MA9	River Bank, Macal	NE Bank, Brown strata
MA10	River Bank, Branch Mouth	West Bank
MO1	River Bank, Mopan	NE Bank, just before Branch Mouth
MO2	River Bank, Mopan	Bullet Tree Falls
MO3	River Bank, Mopan	Bullet Tree Falls
MO4	River Bank, Mopan	West of Branch Mouth
BZ1	River Bank, Belize River	South Bank, near ferry and site of Baking Pot.
BZ2	River Bank, Belize River	North Bank, East of 1st river island
BZ3	Bank, Belize River, Creek	West Bank, creek entrance
BZ4	Bank, Belize River, Creek	West Bank, creek entrance
BZ5	Bank, Belize River	Zone "E" E100, as per survey
MG1	Benque Viejo, Magaña	Benque Viejo
MG2	Happy Home, Magaña	Happy Home, Valley of Peace
MG3	Succotz, Magaña	San Jose Succotz, Near school
MG4	San Antonio Village, Magaña	San Antonio
MG5	Stann Creek, Magaña	Stann Creek
MG6	Succotz, Magaña	Near San Jose Succotz
MG7	Succotz, Magaña	Near San Jose Succotz, Waterhole Road
MG8	Succotz, Magaña	San Jose Succotz
MG9	Succotz, Magaña	Sherd waster

Table 4.1 Raw Materials Samples List with Location and Context

Included in my survey strategy for raw material sources. Local pottery makers were sought since I felt that they would be able to help me locate useable tempers and clays. Plastic containers have largely replaced ceramic vessels, thus the need for modern day potters is virtually non-existent in Belize. However, with a burgeoning tourism industry, there have been efforts to revive pottery making to provide items for sale as souvenirs. At the village of San Jose Succotz, located within my research area, on the southern banks of the Mopan River, Mr. David Magaña has established a workshop called Magaña's Art Gallery and Xunantunich Association. I visited and interviewed Mr. Magaña on two different occasions. Mr. Magaña spoke of the difficulties he had encountered in finding suitable and consistent materials sources. All of his clay sources have been found through his own trial and error experimentation. Neighbours and friends in the process of digging for latrines and septic tanks have aided in the discovery many of his clay sources.

Mr. Magaña generously provided me samples of locally mined tempers and clays he used to produce his pottery wares, as well as samples of clays he had obtained from farther afield that he was planning to test fire to determine whether these new clays were suitable for regular use. Mr. Magaña listed criteria such as survival during the firing process and the production of preferred colourations as important factors in his selection process. Sherds from kiln wasters were also collected to obtain a sample of his finished wares.

All of Mr. Magaña's pots were what archaeologists might consider fine wares typically used in serving and presentation functions. All of the pots were unslipped and burnished or self-slipped. Hand-building and burnishing pottery techniques used by Mr. Magaña in the production of his vessels are similar to those that might have been employed by the ancient Maya so it was with special interest that I included samples from his workshops in my materials study. Mr. Magaña did express that he hoped in future to develop slips for the pottery instead of the acrylic paint used on some of the presentation pieces. Most of his clientele were vacationing tourists; however, some of his unslipped burnished bowls have begun to appear in local restaurants as salsa bowls and ashtrays. Coarser wares, such those for cooking or food and water storage were not part of Mr. Magaña's repertoire.

I asked Mr. Magaña whether there were any other local potters to be found. Mr. Magaña lamented the general lack of community interest in pottery production as people have failed to see pottery making as a viable economic venture. He confirmed my research findings that there were no other pottery makers in the region.

Raw materials samples were exported from Belize to Canada along with the ceramic samples with an export license (No. 284/10/97) from the Belize Department of Archaeology, Ministry of Tourism and the Environment, Belmopan, Belize and a soil import permit from Agriculture and Agri-food Canada #16708 and permit #189942 from Canada Customs. The raw material samples were then prepared for thin sectioning and analyzed in similar fashion to sherd thin sections at the Royal Ontario Museum after inspection from Agriculture and Agri-Food Canada for this specific purpose. The results of these analyses are presented in the raw materials section of chapter five after the petrofabric descriptions.

Figure 4.6 Mr. David Magaña's Pottery Workshop, Succotz, Cayo District, Belize.

Figure 4.7 Mr. David Magaña holds a stone use for pottery burnishing

5

Petrographic Descriptions

Petrofabrics & Nomenclature

Ceramic samples sharing the same petrographic characteristics can be defined in a group distinct from other samples. These groupings are referred to as petrofabrics (Mason 1994:20). The petrofabric definitions that follow in the rest of this chapter provide attribute information that is the basis of comparison of samples.

The naming system for petrofabrics used in this study simply adopts the name of the most abundant mineral element or elements in the petrofabric such as calcite or granite. A sequential numerical designation as also assigned to account for multiple petrofabrics with similar minerals; thus, type names such as "Calcite 1" and "Calcite 2" were created.

It is hoped that with further investigation, beyond the scope of my present study, the naming system devised by Mason (1994:20-21) may be applied in future. Mason's nomenclature system is dependent on evidence, such as excavated kiln wasters, that suggests a petrofabric originated at a specific site and those petrofabrics are named after that site. Petrofabrics that cannot be attributed to a site by securely provenanced ceramics are provisionally named after the site using quotation marks where they were first petrographically defined. For my study, there were no wasters or samples that enabled me to attribute them as produced at a site. Research into locating actual production sites can remedy this situation, not to mention addressing many more questions about economic production and distribution.

Mineral Abundance

In my study, I express the quantity or abundance of each mineral observed in the thin section as a percentage of the total ceramic body. To arrive at this percentage I visually compared the mineral elements in my thin sections with charts that visually illustrate different percentages. These charts were developed for this purpose by Terry and Chillingar (1955). This technique is favoured over word only descriptions such as "abundant" or "scarce" that commonly have no defined values.

Others performing petrographic studies such as Angelini (1998:136-138) have used the point counting technique

for determining the percentage of inclusions within a thin section. Point counting involves identifying and counting any inclusion or void that appears under the crosshairs of the microscope when the sample is moved along at regular intervals until a fixed number of counts are achieved. Counts for each mineral element are then calculated as a percentage from the fixed total number of observations made. Adopted from geological methods designed to provide measurement on areas of thin sectioned rock samples, point counting archaeological ceramic samples may raise questions as to statistical validity. To obtain relevant values geologists will count up to one thousand counts in one rock sample in thin section. Angelini (1998:136-138) used 192 counts on each thin section sample in her study. Archaeologists may find that the large amount of clay matrix in their ceramic samples does not permit the taking of a thousand counts on any one mineral component of a petrofabric (Mason 1994:12). The issue of point counting ceramic thin sections have been raised by Freestone (1991) who observed that wide variation in grain sizes made determination of an appropriate counting interval difficult. Although point counting may give the impression of greater objectivity, it has been noted that "[t]hese measurements are time-consuming, tedious and tiring for the operator and accuracy and precision are likely to depend on a strong subjective element" (Middleton, Freestone and Leese 1985:64). Use of the comparative technique has been advocated for application in the analysis of ceramic material; "[t]his *comparative* process may sound less than precise, but is in fact sufficiently accurate within the variability of any production centre...." (Mason 1994:11-12, Italics mine.)

Granulometry

Textural analyses study the size and shape of non-plastic inclusions in order to characterize and discriminate between possible petrofabrics. Included in textural analyses is the observation of grain size as an attribute in the description of a petrofabric. Size of mineral grains within a ceramic body influences aspects of clay plasticity during the manufacturing process making the clay easier to work. Grain size also affects the strength and heat conduction properties of the finished vessel. In the following descriptions, grain size is expressed as in Table 5.1 after Folk (1980).

Another granulometric attribute used in petrofabric descriptions is the degree of sorting of a given mineral. Sorting can be defined as the range of grain sizes in a petrofabric. "Well sorted" describes inclusions that are uniform in grain size while "poorly sorted" describes inclusions that have a wide range of grain sizes. Figure 5.1 is a comparison chart derived from mathematically calculated parameters acknowledged by sedimentologists (Pettijohn 1987).

Value	Description
>2mm	Grit
1 – 2mm	Very coarse sand
0.5 – 1mm	Coarse sand
0.25 – 0.5mm	Medium sand
0.125 – 0.25mm	Fine sand
0.0625 – 0.125mm	Very fine sand

Table 5.1 Grain Size Description Terms and Values

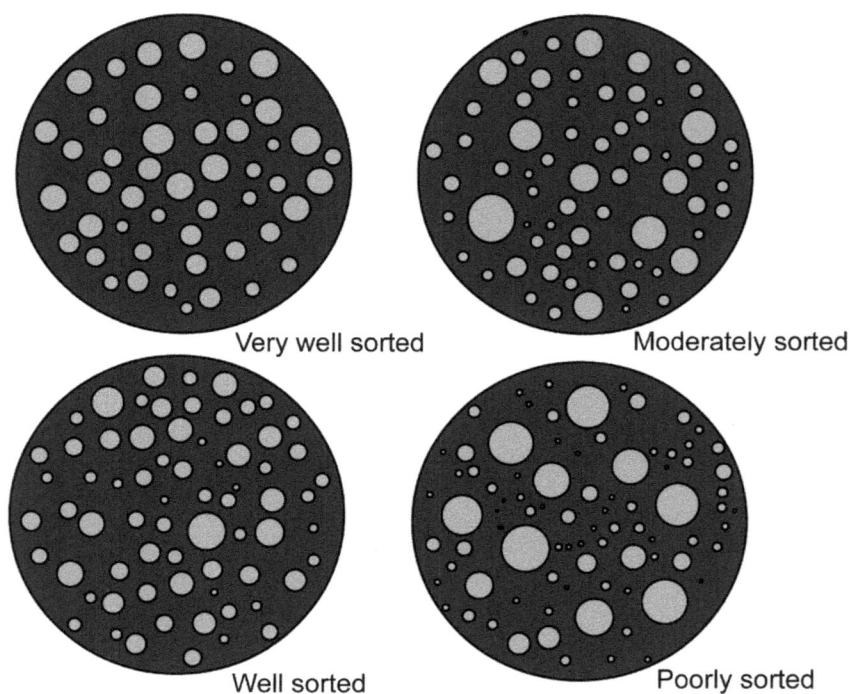

Figure 5.1 Sorting Chart Mason (2004) after Pettijohn et al (1987).

The degree of roundedness is the third granulometric attribute used in petrofabric description. Roundedness refers to the degree of wear on edges of inclusions. In the descriptions roundedness will be described in terms as listed in Table 5.2. For a visual comparison chart please refer to Figure 5.2. (Mason 2004, adapted from Pettijohn 1987).

Roundedness	Description
Angular	Freshly broken, sharp jagged edges
Sub-angular	Some wear on corners
Sub-rounded	Greater wear of edges, rounded but with angular aspects
Rounded	Almost completely rounded
Well-rounded	Completely rounded

Table 5.2 List of Terms Used in Description of Roundedness.,

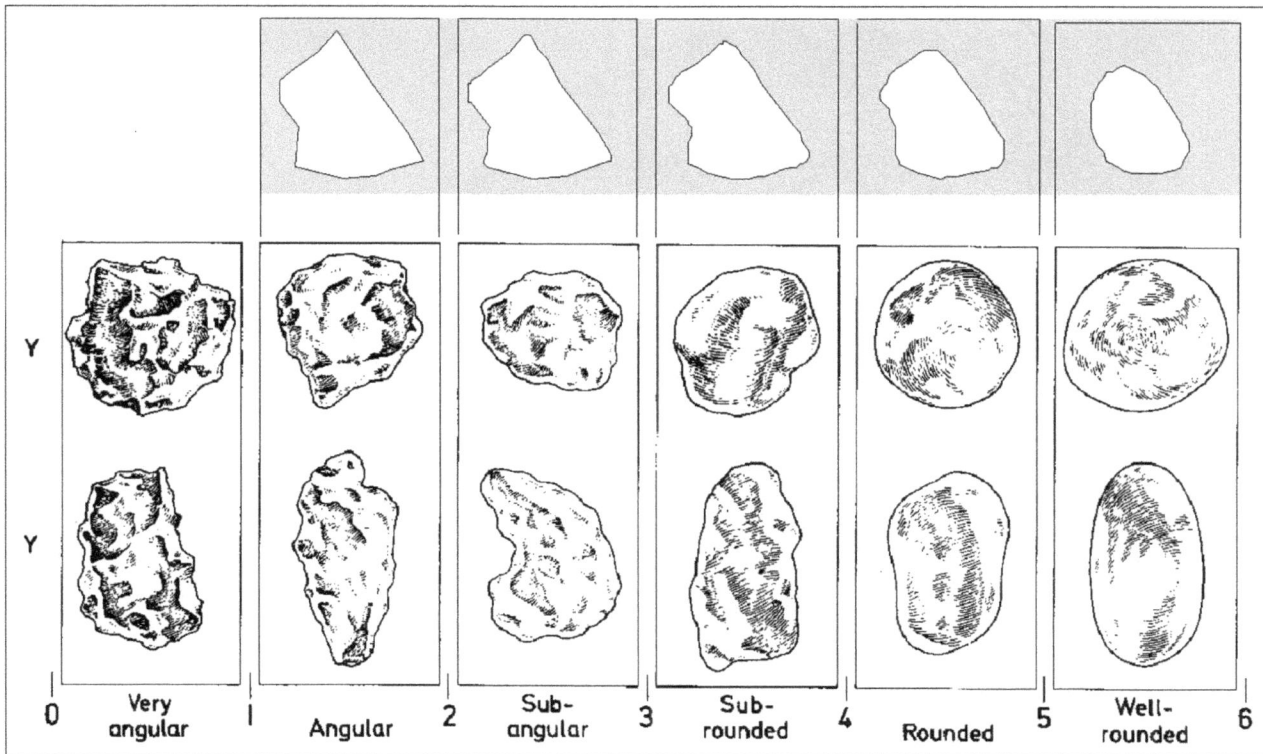

Figure 5.2 Roundedness description chart, Mason (2004) after Pettijohn et al (1987)

Petrofabric Descriptions

"VOLCANIC ASH 1"

- **Overview**

"Volcanic Ash 1" is the first of two petrofabrics found in the Belize Valley containing volcanic ash as its primary non-plastic component. Vessels appear to be all serving or presentation type forms such as plates, vases, and bowls. All sites included in this investigation have yielded ample quantities of this petrofabric.

Vitreous volcanic ash fragments have been observed in this petrofabric to be occasionally imbedded in clumps of micritic calcite, opening the possibility that the ash may have been included as part of limestone beds during their formation. The possibility exists that the ash may have been purposefully mined or collected as it weathered out from such limestone beds.

Type-varieties defined by Gifford (1976) from the Spanish Lookout ceramic complex associated with this petrofabric include Belize Red, Platon Punctate Incised, Chunhitz Orange, Xunantunich Black on Orange, and Benque Viejo Polychrome.

- **Macroscopic Paste Description**

Fabric is porous, soft and friable, uniform in appearance with few visible inclusions, colour varies widely from very pale browns to the whole range of buff, Munsell:

10YR 6/6 - 7/3, 7.5YR 6/4 - 7/4. There is frequent zonation of paste colour with including partially oxidized examples.

- **Petrographic Description**

Overall, the petrofabric is characterised by a fine, homogenous appearance, with vitreous volcanic ash composing 35% to 50% of the paste. The volcanic ash is angular to sub angular in form and is well to very well sorted. Occasional ash fragments (1%) exhibit vesicular forms, similar to pumice stone. The typical grain size for the volcanic ash ranges from fine sand at the smallest to medium sand. Clumps of ash fragments also occur, but actual grain size remains the same. Ash is fresh and glassy and shows no sign of devitrification (see Figures 5.3 and 5.4).

Also present in the petrofabric is biotite mica, 1% to 3%. Typically, the biotite laminae are translucent and sub rounded to rounded in form. Biotite is moderately sorted and of fine to medium sand in grain size.

Quartz inclusions from 5% to 15% are usually moderate to well sorted and sub angular to sub rounded. Quartz grain size is predominantly of fine sand with occasional grains of medium sand.

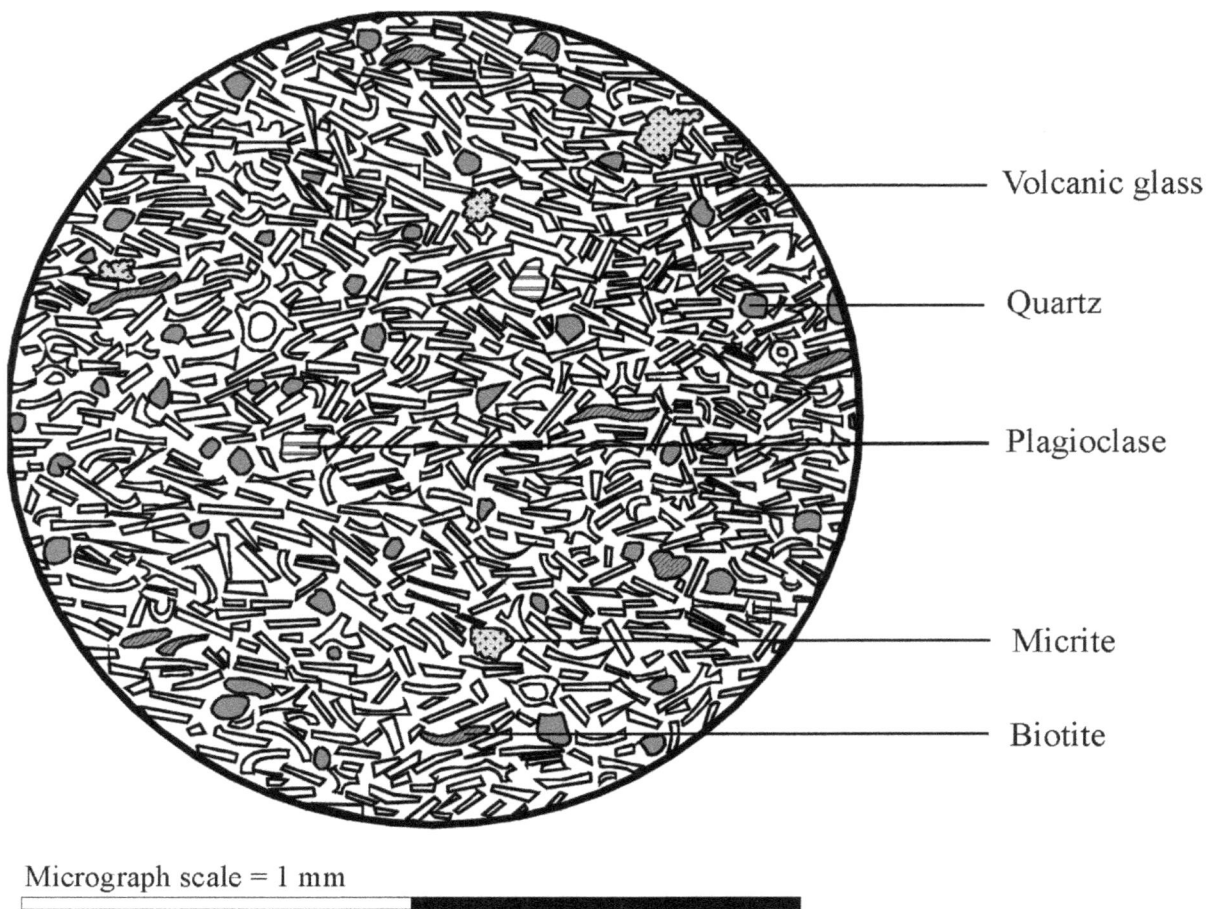

Micrograph scale = 1 mm

Figure 5.3 Line Drawing of "Volcanic Ash 1" Petrofabric

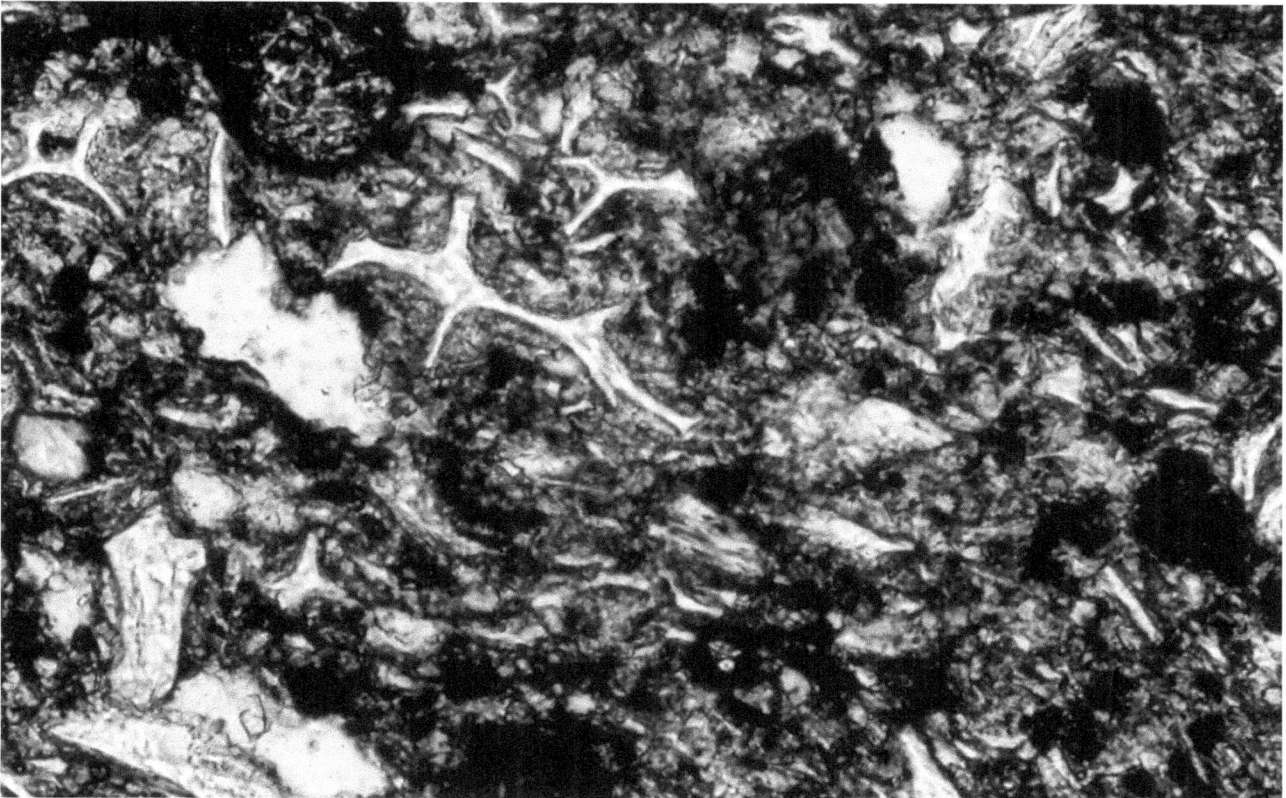

*Figure 5.4 Photomicrograph of "Volcanic Ash 1" Petrofabric under Plain Polarized Light
Field of view approximately 0.5 mm*

Plagioclase feldspar is also a characteristic inclusion varying from 1% to 3%, being moderately sorted and sub angular to sub rounded. Polysynthetic albite twinning is typical of the vast majority plagioclase inclusions. Instances of plagioclase in euhedral crystal form do occur, but very rarely, only in trace quantities being of fine sand in size.

Micritic calcite is observed in trace quantities to a maximum of 1%. Micrite is usually moderate to poorly sorted, of fine sand and rounded to well rounded in shape.

Opaque brown-red inclusions occur sporadically in trace quantities. Opaques are moderate to poorly sorted, rounded to well rounded, and of medium sand grain size.

"VOLCANIC ASH 2"
- **Overview**

The second petrofabric containing volcanic ash was notable with the addition of calcite inclusions. The crystalline calcite is either a local addition to the volcanic ash mixture or possibly a less refined version of the volcanic ash if such ash was mined from limestone beds (please refer to the previous discussion found in "Volcanic Ash 1" overview). "Volcanic Ash 2" is found in smaller quantities than "Volcanic Ash 1" at the sites of Cahal Pech, Xunantunich, Baking Pot, El Pilar and Ontario Village.

Type-varieties defined by Gifford (1976) from the Spanish Lookout ceramic complex associated with this petrofabric include Belize Red, Platon Punctate Incised, and Xunantunich Black on Orange, Gallinero Fluted and Pabellon Modelled-Carved. All vessel forms are of presentation or serving functions such as plates, vases and bowls.

- **Macroscopic Description**

Porous, soft and friable, this petrofabric contains visible crystalline calcite inclusions. Frequent partial oxidization provides for wide colour ranges within a single sample, buff light brown to reddish yellow, Munsell 7.5YR 6/4, 7.5YR 7/6.

- **Petrofabric Description**

Overall, "Volcanic Ash 2" is less uniform, more poorly sorted than "Volcanic Ash 1." The vitreous fragments of volcanic ash in the "Volcanic Ash 2" petrofabric is well to very well sorted, of angular to sub-angular form, ranging from fine to medium sand grain size comprising from 35% to 50% of the paste. The nature of the volcanic ash inclusions in this petrofabric is similar to that of "Volcanic Ash 1" defined previously.

Crystalline calcite inclusions are present in 3% to 10%, and are predominantly of medium sand with the rare sample with coarse grains. Calcite inclusions span a large range of shape from sub angular to rounded. Unlike all the other components in this petrofabric, calcite inclusions are poor to moderately sorted.

Quartz, 1% to 7%, is of medium to fine sand, sub rounded and moderately to well sorted. Biotite mica is found in quantities of trace (<1%) to 3%, generally of fine to medium sand and moderately sorted. Plagioclase feldspar, in quantities of trace to 2%, is found to be of fine sand and moderately sorted.

Volcanic Glass

Calcite

Plagioclase

Quartz

Biotite

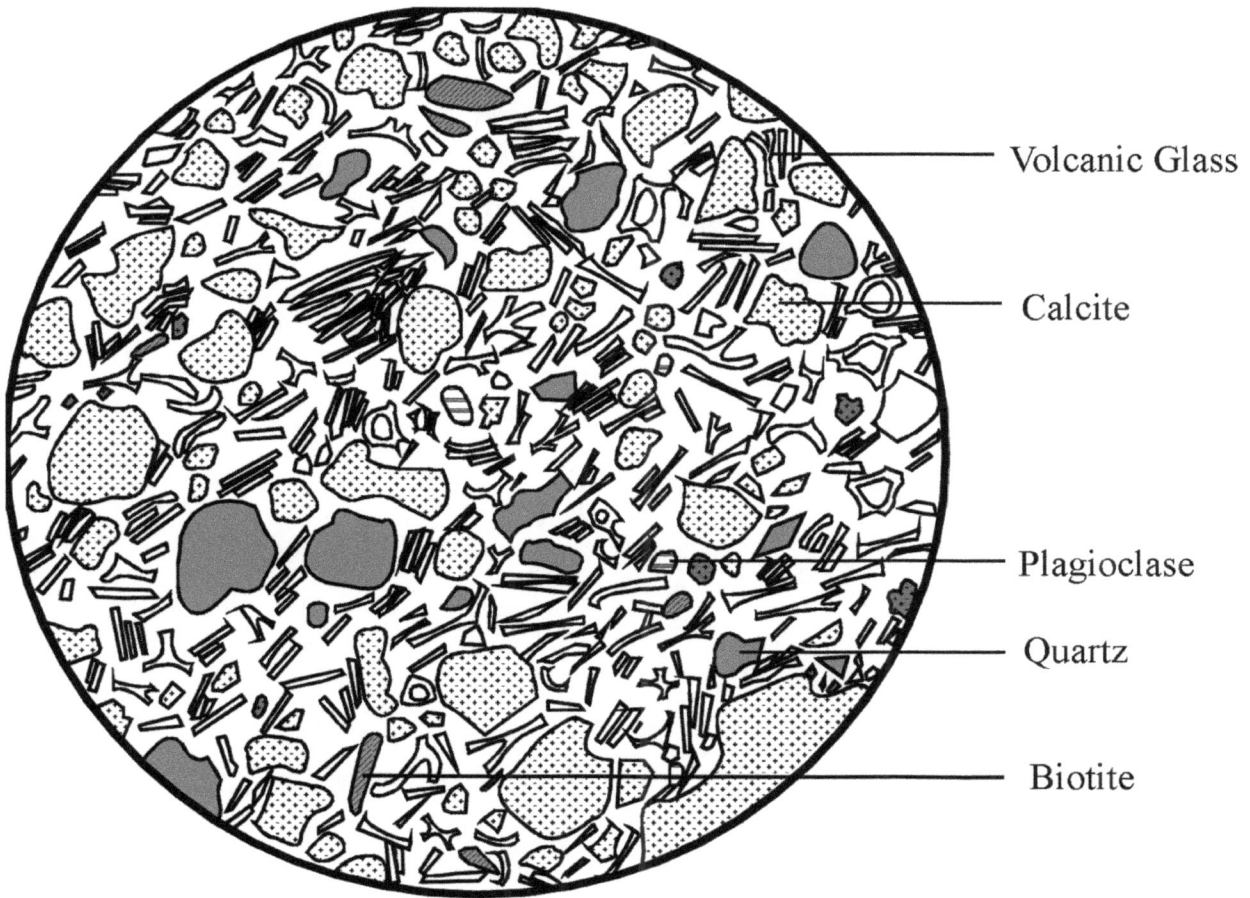

Micrograph scale = 1 mm

Figure 5.5 Line Drawing of "Volcanic Ash 2" Petrofabric

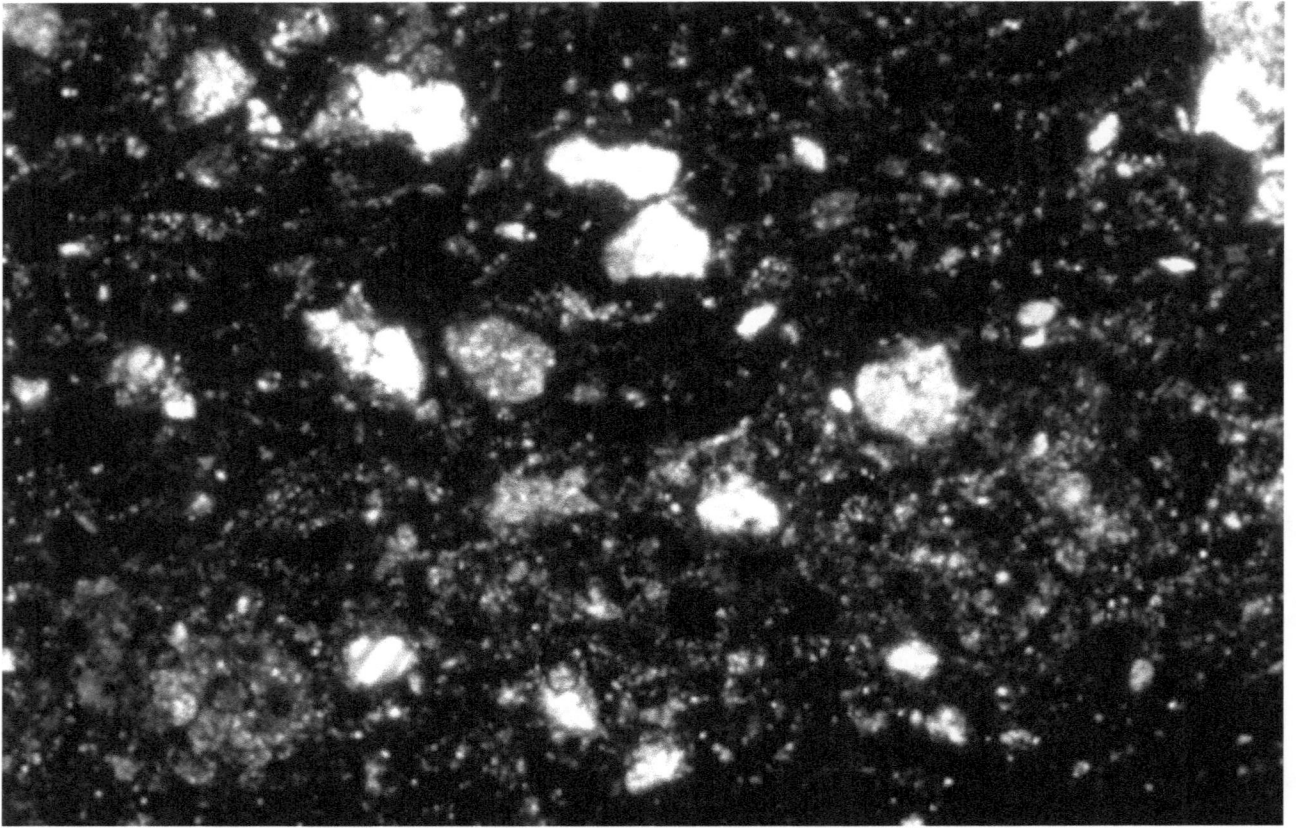

Figure 5.6 Photomicrograph of "Volcanic Ash 2" Petrofabric under Cross Polarized Light
White grains are calcite, volcanic ash is black.
Field of view approximately 1.25 mm

"CALCITE 1"

- **Overview**

Most prevalent forms include bowls and dishes with rare jar forms. Fine to medium sand crystalline calcite grains produce a ceramic well suited for serving and display functions. Larger forms, such as jars, requiring greater structural support in both manufacturing and end use are necessarily rare.

"Calcite 1" is found at all sites within this study. Type-varieties defined by Gifford (1976) from the Spanish Lookout ceramic complex associated with this petrofabric include Mount Maloney Black, Dolphin Head Red, and Garbutt Creek Red.

- **Macroscopic Description**

Fired clay matrix with medium to fine grained calcite inclusions. Vessel wall thickness is usually measured at <10mm. Paste colour varies widely from orange, light brown to reddish yellow, Munsell exterior margin: 7.5YR 6/4, interior margin: 5YR 6/6. Commonly these vessels are slipped; however, preservation of the slip is often poor.

- **Petrographic Description**

Crystalline calcite, medium to fine sand, of angular to sub-angular shape composes approximately 35% of inclusions. The defining characteristic of this petrofabric concerns the granulometry of the calcite inclusions.

Grain size, and sorting of the calcite, are especially diagnostic.

Quartz is present in trace to 20%. Grain size for quartz is of medium to fine sand. Grains are usually sub rounded in form. Sorting ranges from moderate to well sorted.

Opaque inclusions, red-brown, fine to medium sand in size, moderate to poorly sorted, rounded to well rounded, occur in the majority of samples in quantities of trace to 3%.

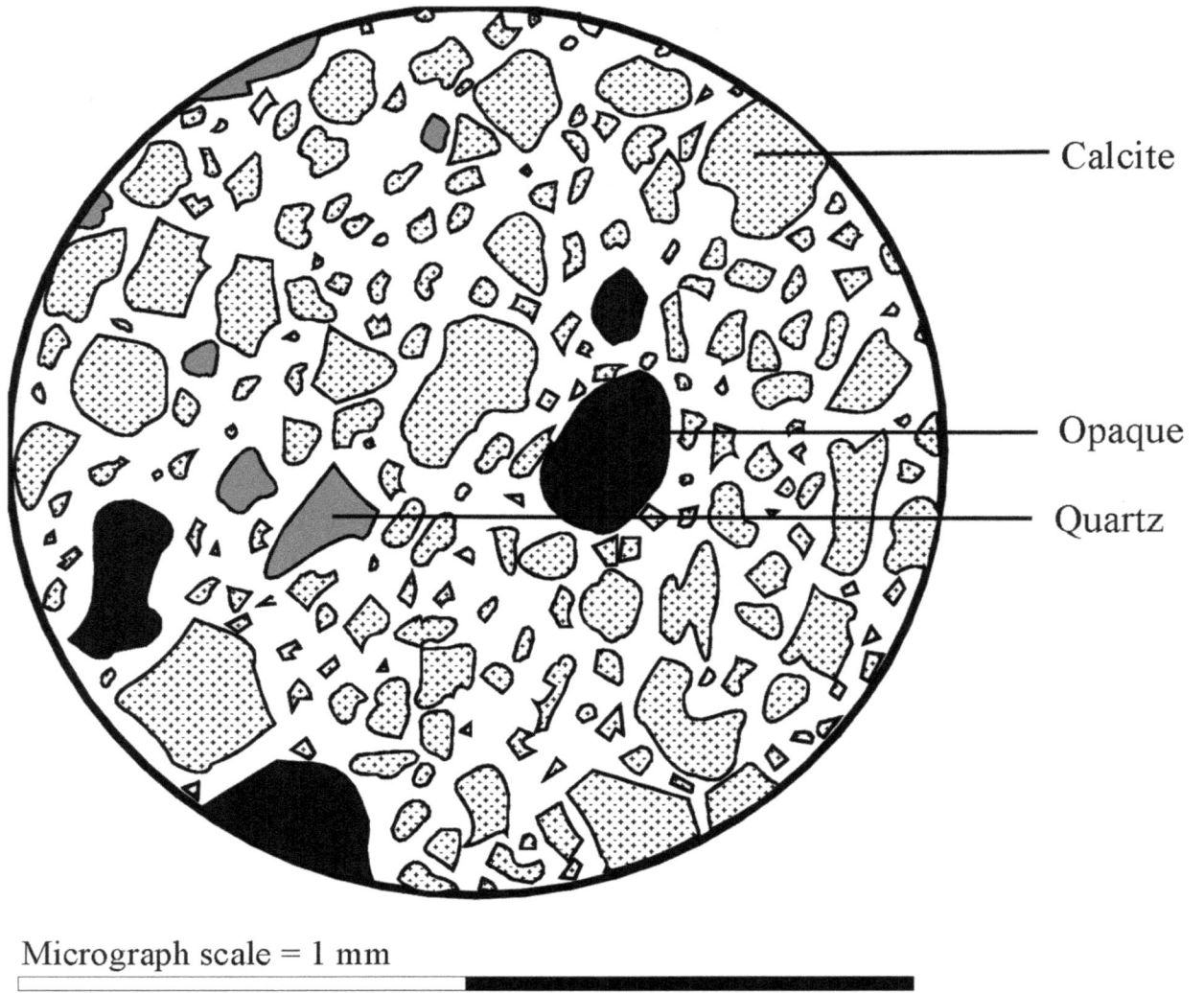

Calcite

Opaque

Quartz

Micrograph scale = 1 mm

Figure 5.7 Line Drawing of "Calcite 1" Petrofabric

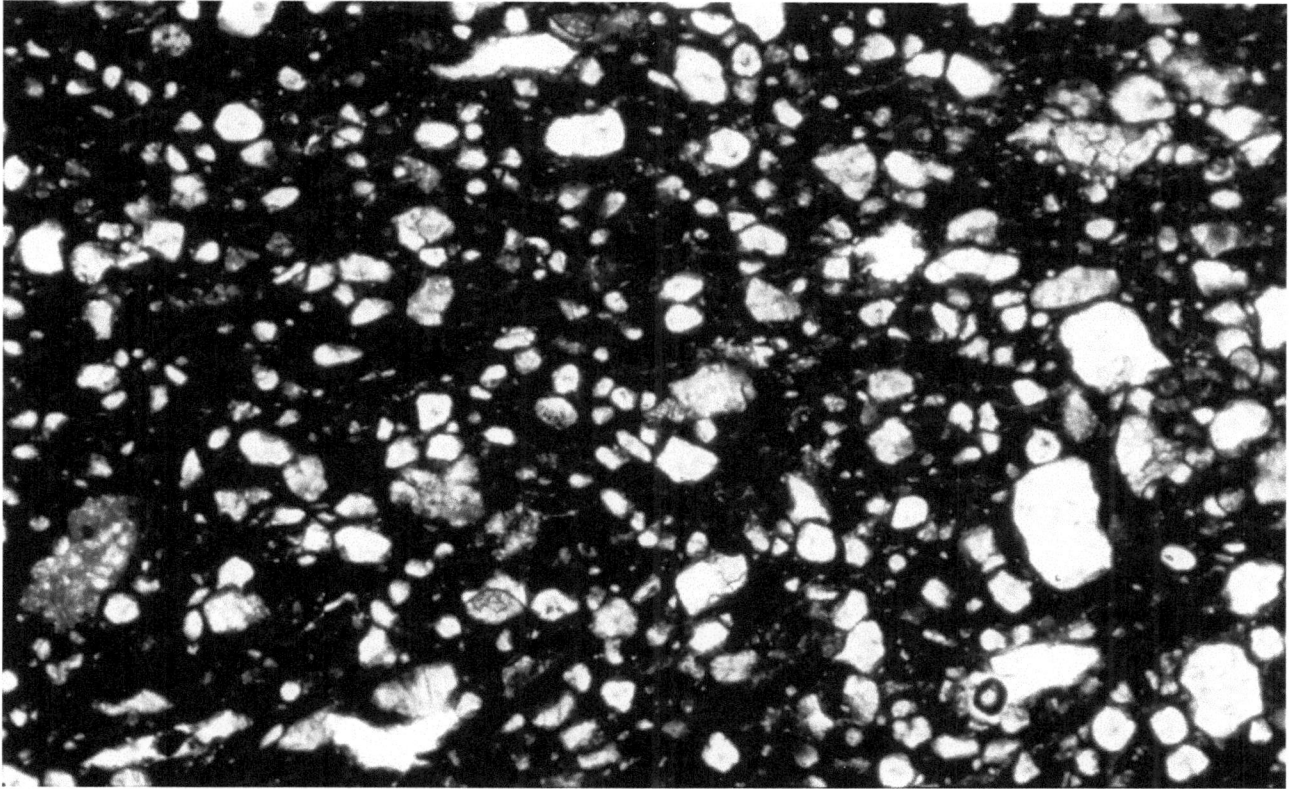

Figure 5.8 Photomicrograph of "Calcite 1" Petrofabric under Plain Polarized Light
Field of view approximately 2 mm

"CALCITE 2"

• Overview

This fabric was found mostly in the large jar or *olla* forms. It is suggested by the high relative abundance of calcite that vessels of this petrofabric were favoured for use in water or food storage rather than cooking. Functions such as cooking that would require subjecting the vessel to high temperatures would destroy calcite inclusions compromising the structural integrity of the vessel. Voids indicating destroyed calcite inclusions are found on both interior and exterior margins of a number of samples. The association of voids with calcite is based on similar shape and distribution. Voids are likely the result of poorly controlled firing in the manufacturing process rather than from fire top cooking over the vessel's use life.

"Calcite 2" petrofabric is widely distributed, found at all sites in this study. Type-varieties defined by Gifford (1976) from the Spanish Lookout ceramic complex associated with this petrofabric include Alexanders Unslipped, Cayo Unslipped and Tu-Tu Camp Striated.

• Macroscopic Description

Fired clay matrix with grit to coarse grained calcite inclusions are generally poorly sorted. The vessel wall had a thickness of 10mm or greater to accommodate for the large grain size of the inclusions. Paste colour varies from light reddish brown to reddish yellow, Munsell, 5YR 6/4, 5YR 6/6.

• Petrographic Description

Crystalline calcite is found in quantities of 55% to a minimum of 20%. The defining attribute of this petrofabric is the grain size of the calcite, grit to very coarse sand. The coarse nature of the calcite distinguishes this petrofabric from "Calcite 1" that has a finer grade of calcite inclusions. Calcite grains vary widely in shape from angular to sub rounded often within a single sample. Sorting of calcite inclusions ranges from moderate to poor. Micritic calcite, trace to 5%, well rounded, is found in conjunction with crystalline calcite. The micrite appears to be deteriorated from the larger calcite grains. Interior and exterior margins of the section may exhibit voids where calcite has been destroyed by high firing or use temperatures.

Hydrochloric acid was used on sections that appeared to contain calcite to determine whether they were in fact calcite. Hydrochloric acid effervesces on calcite. It does not effervesce on samples of dolomite (another type of carbonate mineral).

Quartz is also observed in all samples in quantities of trace to 20%. Predominantly sub rounded in form, quartz grains are of medium to coarse sand in size.

Opaque inclusions are present, coloured red-brown, medium to coarse in size, moderate to poorly sorted, and rounded in form. Opaques occur in the majority of samples in quantities of trace to 3%.

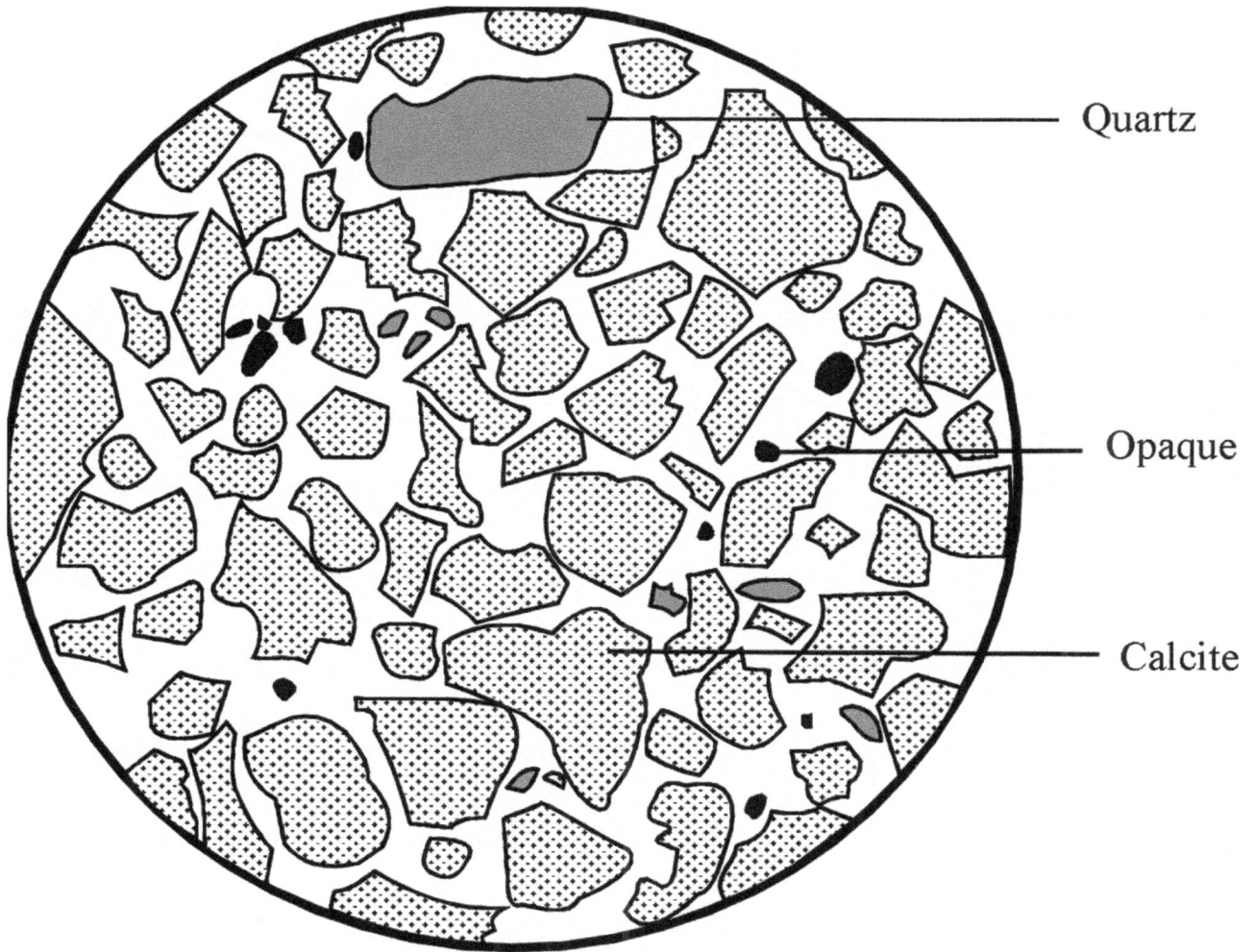

Figure 5.9 Line Drawing of "Calcite 2" Petrofabric

Figure 5.10 Photomicrograph of "Calcite 2" Petrofabric under Cross Polarized Light
Field of view approximately 1.25 mm

"GRANITE 1"

• Overview

"Granite 1" is popular among the jar forms to the near exclusion of other vessel forms. Only rare instances of red and black slipped bowls have been identified as being made of this petrofabric. Containing mineral inclusions that are the base constituents of granite rock, this petrofabric has been found in larger relative frequencies at the site of Baking Pot located right on the banks of the Belize River. Pottery raw materials sourcing performed in the 1997 field season found sand fitting this description deposited along the banks of the Belize River including areas in the direct vicinity of Baking Pot. Granitic inclusions were not found among samples from sites father away from the river system, where calcite limestone was predominant. Sherds of "Granite 1" petrofabric were found at much lower frequencies at the sites of Pacbitun and El Pilar.

Type-varieties defined by Gifford (1976) from the Spanish Lookout ceramic complex associated with this petrofabric include Cayo Unslipped, Alexanders Unslipped, Tu-Tu Camp Striated, Mount Maloney Black and Dolphin Head Red.

• Macroscopic Description

Fired clay matrix, with moderate to poorly sorted grit to coarse sized quartz and feldspar grains. "Granite 1" is often difficult to distinguish from "Calcite 2" since the large quartz and feldspar grains can be mistaken for crystalline calcite using only macroscopic observation.

• Petrofabric Description

Quartz occurs in frequencies of 5% to 25% and is poor to moderately sorted. Quartz inclusions are sub angular to sub rounded. Grains are medium to very coarse sand. In all samples of quartz are found to have undulose extinction and are also polycrystalline in structure.

Alkali potassic feldspars, orthoclase, and microcline are found in "Granite 1." Microcline ranges from trace frequencies to 10%, while orthoclase can be found ranging from 1% to 7%. Feldspars are poorly sorted and are sub rounded to rounded in form. Grain size varies from grit to coarse sand.

Quartz and feldspar inclusions tend to looked weathered and, in some cases, are slightly altered. This suggests that inclusions in this petrofabric are derived from sands that are the result of the erosion of granite. Weathered granites compose the Maya Mountains and the Mountain Pine Ridge areas that are drained by the Macal River tributary of the Belize River system.

Micas are also found in the form of biotite and muscovite. Laminae of both types of mica are sub rounded to rounded, are poor to moderately sorted, and grain size ranges from fine to medium sand.

Opaque inclusions, brown to black in colour, are found moderate to poorly sorted in frequencies of 1% to 5%. These opaques are rounded to very well rounded and coarse to medium sand in size.

Very occasionally, crystalline calcite and micritic calcite are found in trace frequencies. Frequencies are too small to enable an observation on the sorting of this inclusion. The calcite is sub rounded to rounded and medium sand in size. The majority of "Granite 1" samples analysed did not contain calcite.

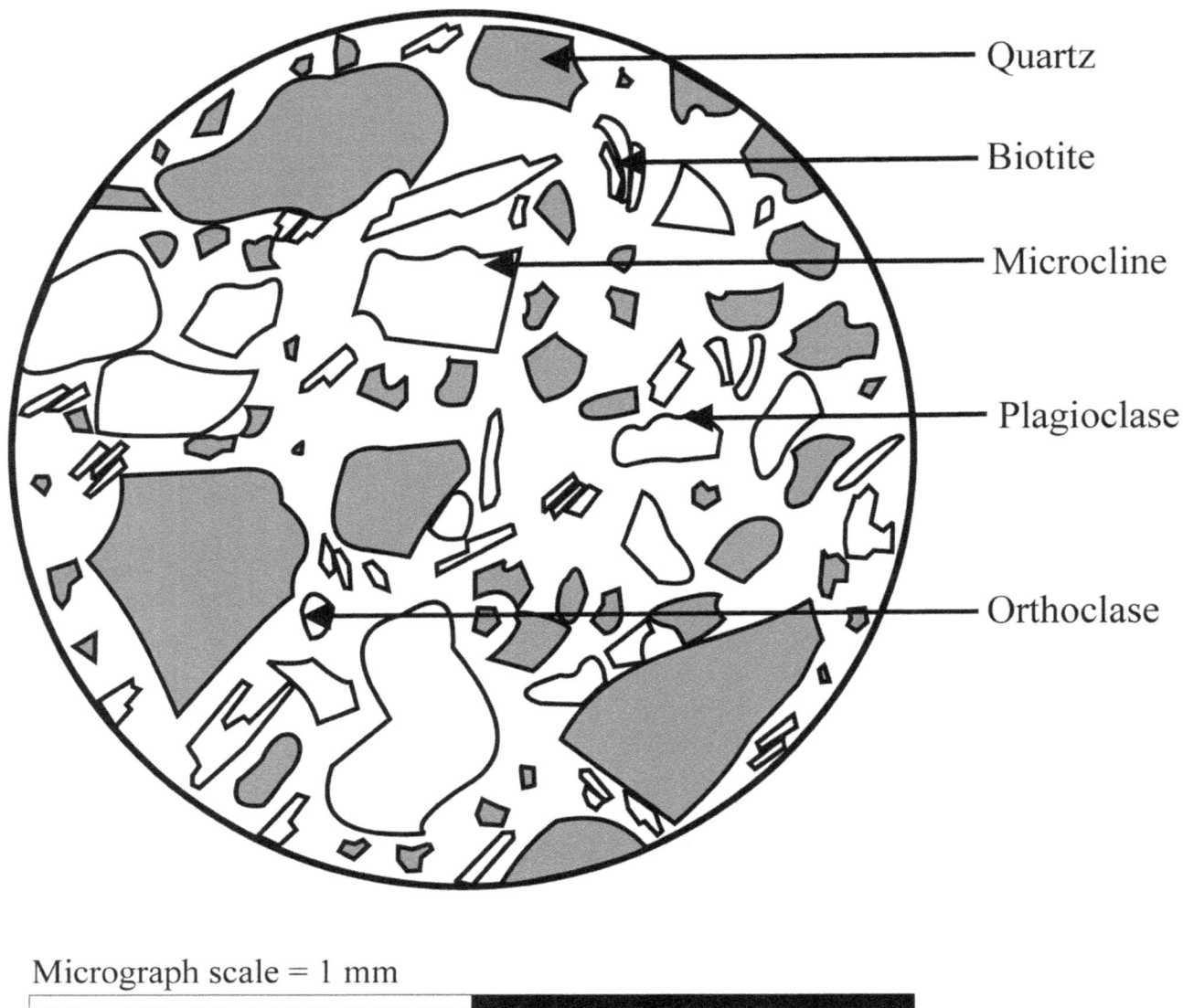

Quartz

Biotite

Microcline

Plagioclase

Orthoclase

Micrograph scale = 1 mm

Figure 5.11 Line Drawing of "Granite 1" Petrofabric

Figure 5.12 Photomicrograph of "Granite 1" Petrofabric under Cross Polarized Light
Field of view approximately 1.25 mm

Figure 5.13 View of the Mountain Pine Ridge, Belize

Petrographic Analysis of Raw Materials Samples

As previously mentioned in Chapter Four, I performed a raw materials sourcing program in the Belize River Valley region. The results of this sourcing are presented in Table 5.3. Many samples, most notably ones from Baking Pot (BP1-3), the Mopan River (MO2-4) and those from David Magaña contained calcite as the primary mineral. The calcite observed in the raw materials samples was consistent with that found in ceramic petrofabric groups "Calcite 1" and "Calcite 2" providing further evidence that these petrofabrics are likely to be locally derived. Calcite and micrite are common mineral elements in most of the samples collected reflecting the underlying local limestone geology.

Raw materials samples from the Macal River (MA1, MA3, and MA9), the cave contexts along the Roaring Creek (AT3-4, UK1-3) and Mopan River (MO1) provide evidence of sand composed of quartz, feldspar and mica. It should be noted that all of these samples were waterborne sands deposited along the banks. Tracing the courses of these river systems they are found to originate in the Mountain Pine Ridge area of west central Belize known to be composed of various granites (see Figure 5.12). Similar granitic mineral elements have been observed in "Granite 1" petrofabric suggesting that this petrofabric can considered as locally derived, made from sands sourced in nearby rivers.

One anomalous sample comes from Laughing Bird Caye, located off the south eastern shore of Belize. Raw materials sampling was not formally conducted in this region, far removed from the Belize River Valley. However, one sample of pumice-like stone was collected due to my interest in finding any evidence of volcanic material in Belize. Thin sectioning of the sample confirmed that it was indeed volcanic pumice, very fresh and glassy. The absence of plagioclase and biotite minerals make this sample compositionally different from the volcanics observed in the ceramic thin sections. This sample may have been carried along rivers originating in southern Guatemala or northern Honduras to be deposited on the offshore cayes but it is impossible to say with any certainty.

All the raw materials sampled were divided into preliminary groups based on location of collection, macroscopically observable textural and mineralogical attributes. Thin sections representative of each of these initial groups were made in a sampling strategy similar to that applied to the ceramics in this study.

Table 5.3 Raw Materials: Macroscopic and Mineralogical Identifications

#	Macroscopic Description	Mineralogical Composition
AT1	Red Clay	Quartz, Muscovite, Biotite
AT2	Sand	Quartz polycrystalline undulose, Biotite, Muscovite, Opaques
AT3	Coarse grained flowstone calcite	Quartz polycrystalline undulose, Biotite, Orthoclase, all encased in micritic:oolithic-like granules
AT4	Sand	Quartz, Biotite, Orthoclase, Microcline, Opaques
AT5	Clay	Not thin sectioned
AT6	Sand and charcoal bits	Calcite with observable crystalline structure, Micrite
UK1	Sand	Quartz, Orthoclase, Granophyre, Perthite
UK2	Clay	Micrite, Crystalline calcite, trace: Quartz, Orthoclase, Biotite, Shell
UK3	Red brown clay	Quartz, Crystalline calcite, Biotite, Orthoclase
UK4	Sand, creamy white, crystalline	Crystalline calcite, trace opaques
YA1	Sand, coarse	Quartz, Biotite, Orthoclase, Opaques
SH1	Sand, fine	Quartz, Muscovite, Biotite, Opaques, Microperthite
SH2	Sand, fine	Quartz, Muscovite, Opaques
BP1	Compact brown. Structural fill	Quartz, Crystalline calcite, Micrite, Opaques, Biotite, Muscovite
BP2	Compact brown. Structural fill	Quartz, Crystalline calcite, Micrite, Opaques, Biotite, Muscovite
BP3	Compact brown. Structural fill	Quartz, Crystalline calcite, Micrite, Opaques, Biotite, Muscovite
LB1	Pumice stone, well rounded	Volcanic glass, Biotite, Quartz, Plagioclase
MA1	Sand	Quartz, Microperthite, Orthoclase, Opaques
#	Macroscopic Description	Mineralogical Composition

MA2	Sand	Not thin sectioned
MA3	Sand	Quartz polycrystalline undulose, Muscovite, Perthite, Plagioclase
MA4	Sand	Not thin sectioned
MA5	Sand	Not thin sectioned
MA6	Pink Clay	Micrite, trace Quartz
MA7	Clear Rock	Not thin sectioned
MA8	Yellow Green Clay	Micrite, Crystalline calcite, trace amounts of Quartz
MA9	Brown Clay	Quartz, Opaques, Muscovite, Calcite, Orthoclase
MA10	White Green Clay	Not thin sectioned
MO1	Grey Brown Clay	Micrite, Calcite, Quartz, Plagioclase, Biotite
MO2	Sand	Micrite, Calcite, Muscovite, Quartz
MO3	Sand	Micrite, Calcite, Quartz, Biotite
MO4	Clay	Micrite, Calcite, Quartz, Biotite
BZ1	Sand, Alluvial Deposit	Quartz, Micrite, Microperthite, Orthoclase
BZ2	Green Brown Clay	Quartz, Plagioclase, Orthoclase, Biotite, Opaques
BZ3	Sand, Alluvial Deposit	Not thin sectioned
BZ4	Green Brown Clay	Not thin sectioned
BZ5	Sand, Alluvial Deposit	Not thin sectioned
MG1	Clay	Quartz
MG2	Clay	Muscovite
MG3	Clay, used for pots	Calcite
MG4	Red Clay	Muscovite, Quartz, Opaques
MG5	Green Clay	Not thin sectioned
MG6	Cal, tempering sand	Micrite, Calcite
MG7	Cal, tempering sand	Micrite, Calcite
MG8	Grog from Succotz Clay	Not thin sectioned

Table 5.3 Continued, Raw Materials: Macroscopic and Mineralogical Identifications

Key
AT = Actun Tunichil Muknal
UK = Uayazaba Kab
YA = Yaxteel Ahau
SH = St. Herman's Cave
BP = Baking Pot
LB = Laughing Bird Caye
MA = Macal River
MO = Mopan River
BZ = Belize River,
MG = David Magaña

6

Analyses and Interpretations

Belize River Valley Ceramic Petrology

The results of petrographic analysis presented in the previous chapter outlined five petrofabrics that have been defined in this study for the Belize River Valley: "Calcite 1", "Calcite 2", "Volcanic 1", "Volcanic 2" and "Granite 1". Three of the five, "Calcite 1," "Calcite 2" and "Granite 1," are petrofabrics compatible with confirmed local geology. The volcanic petrofabrics are indicative of non-local geology. What follows is a discussion of each of the petrofabric types framing them in the context of the Belize River Valley region. Emphasis will be on the significance and role of these types for the regional economy during the Late Classic period. Figure 6.1 illustrates the distribution of the petrofabrics by site.

Locally Derived Petrofabrics:

"Calcite 1" and "Calcite 2"
Both calcite petrofabrics were present at all sites in the sample. "Calcite 1" is the petrofabric found in serving vessels, taking the form of bowls and plates. "Calcite 1" petrofabric forms 25.5% of the ceramic assemblage when averaged from the sites in my study. Pacbitun had the lowest percentage of "Calcite 1" at 13%, while Ontario Village had the highest rate at 44%, (see Figure 6.2).

"Calcite 2" is represented predominantly by jar or *olla* forms with storage, cooking and water vessel functions. "Calcite 2" petrofabric represents an average of 41% of the total ceramic assemblage at the eight sites sampled for this study. Ontario Village had the smallest percentage of "Calcite 2" at 31%, while Blackman Eddy had the highest at 54% (see Figure 6.2).

It has been suggested by Sheppard that the calcites identified in ceramics from San Jose, located 14 miles north of the Belize River on Wamil Creek, are derived from geologically recent carbonates (limestone). Sheppard (1939:272) described an "...almost pure carbonate which has occasionally a red tinge due to traces of iron..." that forms the bedrock of the region. This (in a geological time scale) recently formed limestone is part of what is referred to by geologists as the Boulder Group of the Cayo Series (Dixon 195625-27), formed in the Miocene (23 to 5 m.y.a.) to present. Calcite petrofabrics examined in this study identify both crystalline and cryptocrystalline (micritic) calcite as does Sheppard (1939:253-256). It is likely that "Calcite 1" and "Calcite 2" petrofabrics are derived from local Cayo Series limestones. However, the use of older Cretaceous (146 to 65 m.y.a.) or Paleocene-Eocene (65 to 54 and 54-38 m.y.a. respectively) limestones located outside of the valley to the north cannot, at this point, be ruled out completely. These earlier limestone formations are characterized by the presence of marine fossils typical of each time period. Although there was no evidence of marine fossils in the calcite observed in thin section, it cannot be assumed that fossils could be identified in the small inclusions typical of the calcite found in pottery.

Beyond the scope of the present investigation, an intensive study on calcite petrofabrics alone, in concert with better geological and mineralogical definition of local limestone deposits, would be able to further characterize these petrofabrics. This type of investigation might allow us to discern distinctions within the "Calcite 1" and "Calcite 2" petrofabrics. These distinctions could be made if different types of calcite with different source locations could be identified. Further splitting of my current petrofabric groups could lead to an even better understanding of distributional patterning and related economic factors.

It could be argued that the wide availability of calcite as a raw material might reflect the selection at different sites of the same materials for similar vessels with production occuring at each individual site. Though this possibility should not be dismissed, it should also be noted that there was not only a high degree of homogeniety and consistency, but also a specialized level of skill displayed in the manufacture of calcite ceramic types. This would lead me to favour the idea that manufacture of calcite ceramics was more regionally centralized rather than being performed on a site to site basis. At present I would posit that the calcite petrofabrics outline a broad regional economy. This is suggested by the extensive distribution of the calcite petrofabrics that are present in large quantities at each site in the studied in the region.

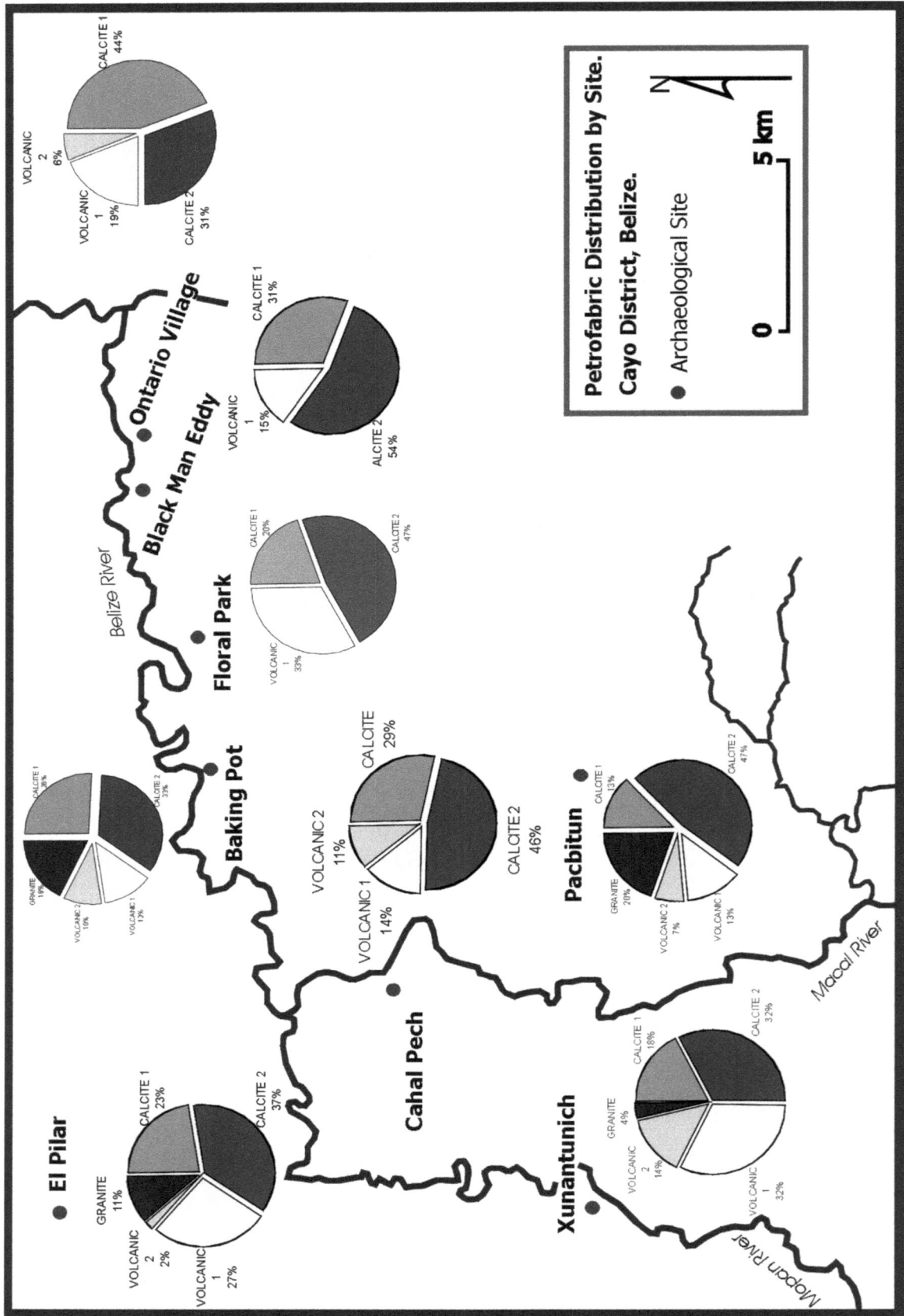

Figure 6.1 Petrographic Distribution by Site, Cayo District, Belize.

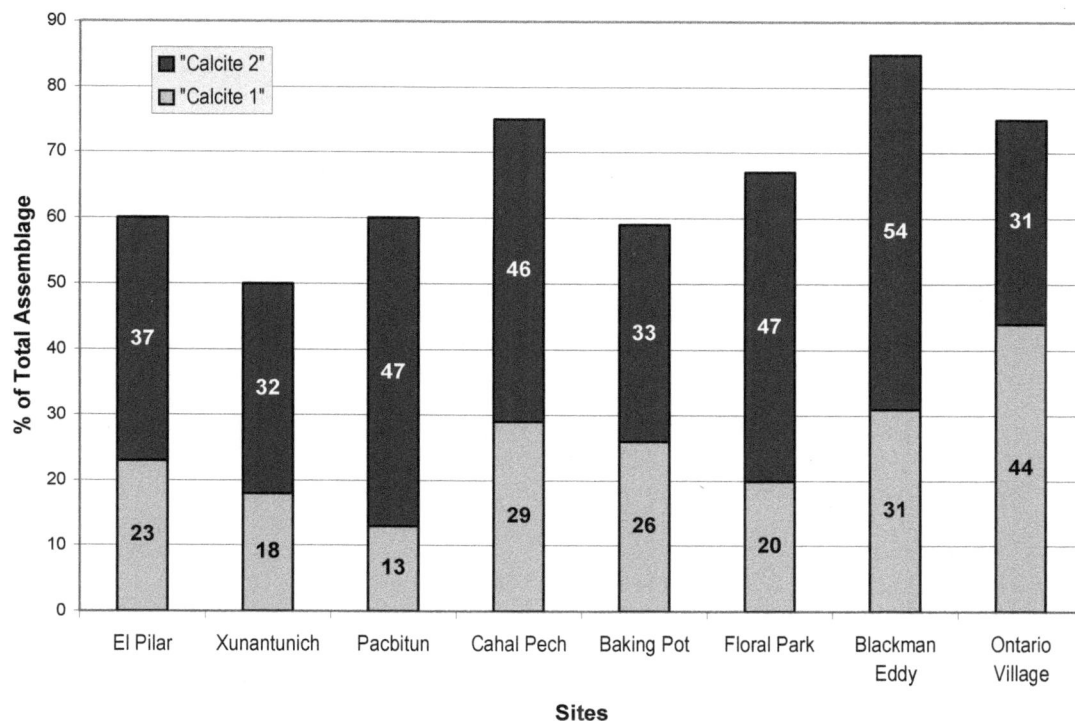

Figure 6.2 Calcite Petrofabrics: Percentage of Total Ceramic Assemblages

	El Pilar	Xunantunich	Pacbitun	Cahal Pech	Baking Pot	Floral Park	Blackman Eddy	Ontario Village
"Calcite 1"	10	5	2	8	16	3	4	6
"Calcite 2"	16	9	7	13	21	7	10	6
Total Sample Size	44	28	15	28	62	15	17	16

Table 6.1 Actual Sample Sizes for "Calcite 1," "Calcite 2" and All Sites

"Granite 1"

The "Granite 1" petrofabric is composed of granitic sands containing quartz, biotite mica and feldspars including microcline and orthoclase. Petrographic analysis of sands and clays sourced by the author along the banks of the Macal, Mopan and Belize Rivers revealed them to be consistent in composition with granites composing the Mountain Pine Ridge Batholith (Shipley 1978:13-48), located along the flanks of the Maya Mountains. These granitic sands are present in the sampled pottery and were found to be easily accessible from prehispanic settlements such as Baking Pot. It should be noted that Pacbitun, located nearest to the batholith formation, had the highest frequency of the "Granite 1" petrofabric at 20% with Baking Pot following closely at 18%, (see below, Figure 6.3).

It is also interesting to observe that only half of the sites tested had "Granite 1" as part of their ceramic assemblages. The sites of Cahal Pech, Floral Park, Blackman Eddy and Ontario Village samples did not include "Granite 1". This may be due to the smaller sample sizes at Floral Park, Blackman Eddy and Ontario Village, but does not explain the absence of "Granite 1" at Cahal Pech where greater access to collections allowed for a generous sample. Despite the possibility of sampling as a deranging factor, it should be noted that Floral Park, Blackman Eddy, and Ontario Village are located to the easternmost extent of the study area. This situates these sites furthest from the source of the granitic sand; additionally, the Belize River in this eastern area meanders much less, with fewer oxbows where sand would be deposited along the riverbanks and rendered accessible to potters.

Sites at which "Granite 1" is found show slightly lower frequencies of both the "Calcite 1" and "Calcite 2" petrofabrics. This phenomenon is most pronounced at the site of Baking Pot. Through a consideration of the formal types involved, "Granite 1" is found in serving vessels and coarser storage/water vessels, the same vessels that "Calcite 1" and "Calcite 2" petrofabrics are associated with in the assemblages at valley sites. It appears that the use of "Granite 1" has partially replaced the use of calcite for similar vessels at the site of Baking Pot. Baking Pot is located on a particularly meandering section of the Belize River where oxbows have formed to the west and east of the site providing an ample source of readily accessible granitic sand.

Based on distributional evidence, it is suggested here that the "Granite 1" petrofabric was locally manufactured in the Belize Valley. Pacbitun and Baking Pot are likely candidates for manufacturing localities of "Granite 1" ceramics, taking into account the high proportions found at these sites. Both Xunantunich and El Pilar are located some distance from sources of granitic sand and it is proposed that these sites were consumers, not producers, of this petrofabric. Xunantunich and El Pilar are prominent sites with large Late Classic components including many areas of ceremonial and administrative function with large plaza areas and monumental architecture surrounded by extensive zones of settlement. Pacbitun and Baking Pot are comparatively smaller sites with less monumental architecture, though with significant settlement areas.

Though specific research to find ceramic production areas has not been performed in the region, previous research at Pacbitun (Healy et al. 1993; Sunahara 1995:106-107) has offered evidence of the working and production of slate objects at mounds located on the site's western periphery. (Slate is a resource local to Pacbitun.) Slate artifacts have been found at sites removed from the Pacbitun area, such as Cahal Pech, thus setting a precedent for the distribution of ceramics suggested here. Xunantunich and El Pilar are the two most socio-politically significant sites in this region that could conceivably have hosted regional markets that would have drawn "Granite 1" ceramics to their inhabitants. It appears that Floral Park, Blackman Eddy, Ontario Village and Cahal Pech did not participate in the distribution sphere for "Granite 1" ceramics. The distribution of "Granite 1" provides insight into what can be described as a local sub-regional economic interaction.

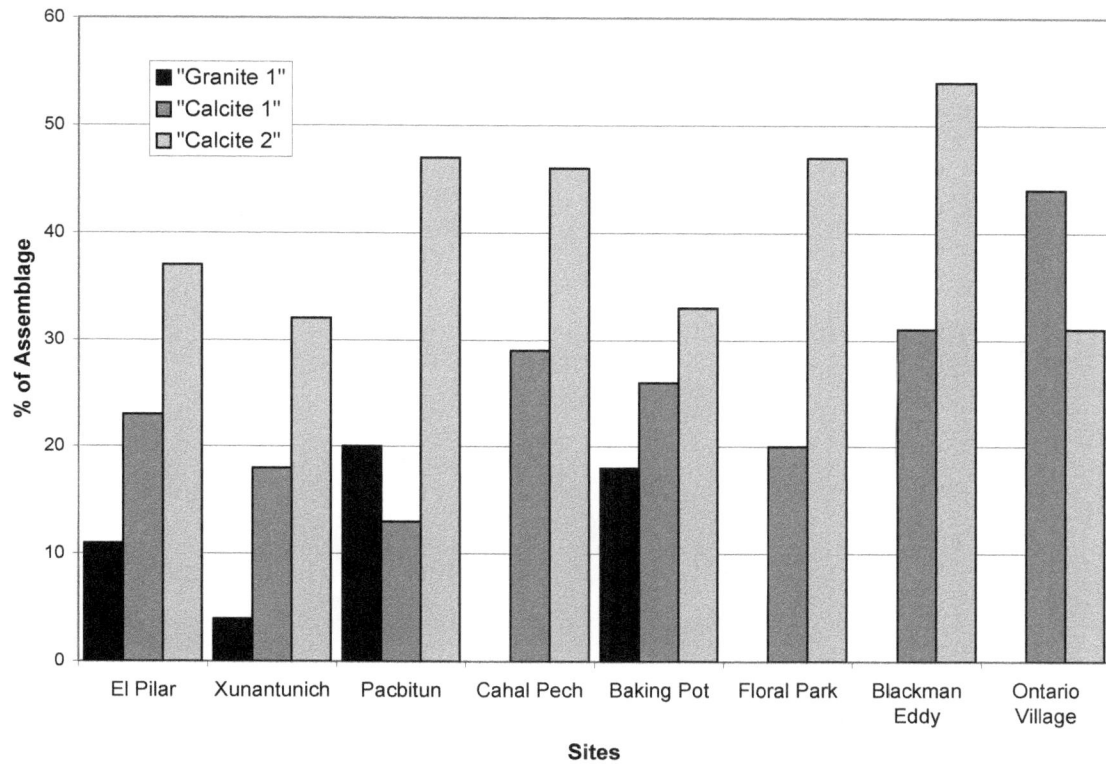

Figure 6.3 "Granite 1" Compared with "Calcite 1" & "Calcite 2" Petrofabrics

	El Pilar	Xunantunich	Pacbitun	Cahal Pech	Baking Pot	Floral Park	Blackman Eddy	Ontario Village
"Calcite 1"	10	5	2	8	16	3	4	6
"Calcite 2"	16	9	7	13	21	7	10	6
"Granite 1"	5	1	3	0	11	0	0	0
Total Sample Size	44	28	15	28	62	15	17	16

Table 6.2 Actual Sample Sizes for "Calcite 1," "Calcite 2, "Granite 1" and All Sites

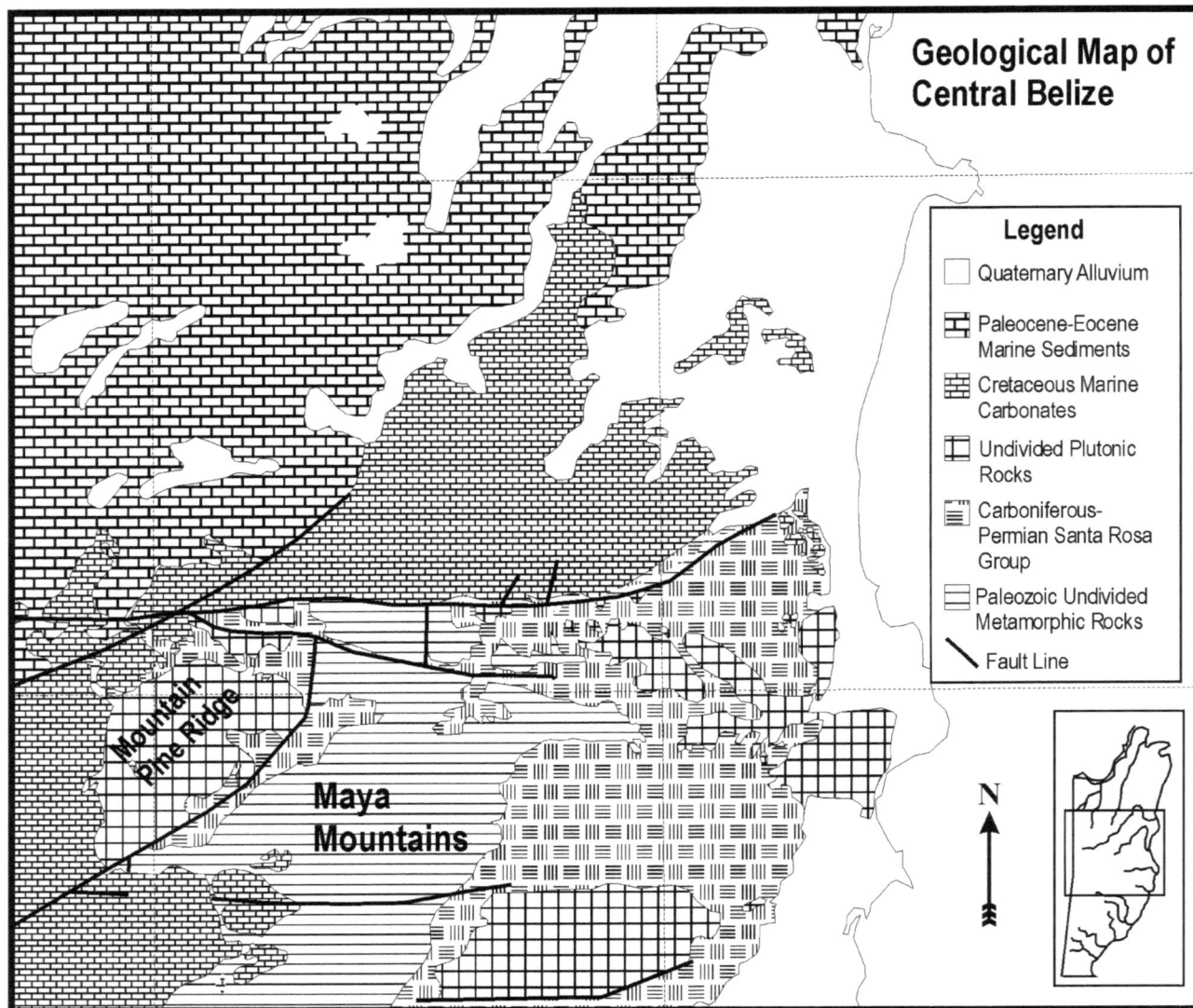

Figure 6.4 Geological Map of Central Belize, (after Bonis and Bohnenberger 1970)

Extraregional Elements in Petrofabrics

The "Volcanic 1" and "Volcanic 2" petrofabrics are more problematic with regard to sourcing a point of origin. There are three possible hypotheses to explain the presence of volcanic ash in Belize Valley ceramics that will be discussed in detail. The first possibility is that there is a local source of ash that was exploited by potters in the valley. A second theory would posit that raw volcanic ash was transported into the valley in bulk amounts and then incorporated into locally manufactured ceramics. The third hypothesis is that finished volcanic ash vessels were made elsewhere and imported into the Belize Valley.

Hypothesis One – Local Volcanic Ash Sources

Evidence of volcanic ash was found neither through the author's raw materials sourcing in the Belize River Valley, nor by the geological fieldwork of Ford and Glicken (1987:494) within Belize. Welded tuff of Paleozoic date (early Pennsylvanian, 325-286 m.y.a.) has been located by Shipley (1978:31-32) to the south of the Mountain Pine Ridge Batholith, in the northern part of the Maya Mountains. The composition of this welded tuff does not correspond with the volcanics found in the ceramic petrofabric. The Paleozoic welded tuff is differentiated from the volcanics found in the ceramics by the presence of alkali feldspar phenocrysts (crystals) such as sanidine. No sanidine was found in the ceramic samples; instead, chemically different plagioclase feldspars were evident, suggesting that the source of the volcanic ash was located elsewhere. Additionally biotite mica, identified in the Belize Valley volcanic petrofabrics, is not present in the Paleozoic welded tuff of the Maya Mountains. (See Figure 6.4)

Upon consultation with a Shari Preece, a volcanologist at the Environmental Sciences Division of Physical Sciences University of Toronto, the ash found in thin-section was described as tephra derived from accumulated ash deposited through distal air fall from a volcanic eruption (pc. Preece 2001). What is commonly referred to as volcanic ash by archaeologists working in the Maya area is more accurately described by volcanologists as tephra. The tuff described by Shipley was welded, not loose like tephra, and proximal to its source being on the periphery of the Pine Ridge Batholith. It is also very unlikely that ash of Paleozoic date would be as clear and glassy as the fresh ash present in the ceramic samples as illustrated in Figure 6.5.

Continuing the search for a source of volcanic ash in the lowlands, Simmons and Brem (1979:84-85) have tested volcanic ash from the Orange Walk District in north-central Belize found in a lens layered within limestone. Their research has revealed that the nature of the ash, highly weathered with a low proportion of glassy fragments (around 5%), is unlike the ash they described

in Northern Yucatan petrofabrics from the sites of Chichen Itza and Dzibilchaltun. Ceramics were tested from the site of Barton Ramie (Simmons and Brem 1979:84-85) in the Belize Valley and were also found not to have originated from the Orange Walk ash lens. Extensive petrographic analyses performed in my study confirm their assertion. "Volcanic 1" and "Volcanic 2" petrofabrics defined in Chapter Five are fresh and not weathered, with proportions of glassy fragments ranging from 35% to 50%, quite different from the 5% of the Orange Walk lens sample. Additionally, biotite mica proportions differ, in the Belize Valley volcanic petrofabrics they are trace to 3%, in contrast to the 30% to 40% in the Orange Walk lens sample.

Sheppard (1939:272) speculated on the wind-borne deposition of volcanic ash lenses in the local limestone of the region. My analyses of the Belize Valley ceramics reveal that volcanic ash petrofabrics compose a significant portion of the ceramic assemblage for the valley at approximately 27% (see Figure 6.1). The homogenous nature of the ash observed in thin-section combined with the high quantities recovered at archaeological sites in the Belize Valley (roughly 43% of the Barton Ramie assemblage) suggest that the source was continuous and reliable. It is therefore questionable that Maya potters were dependent on unpredictable wind carried ash deposits.

Ford and Glicken (1987) have examined the issue of volcanic ash in ceramics of the central Maya lowlands using samples from the Tikal-Yaxha and Yaxha-Sacnab areas in Guatemala. Considering the observed lack of differential access to ash tempered vessels based on factors of wealth, status, and distance from site cores, Ford and Glicken propose that a lowland local source for the ash would best account for the large quantity of volcanic ash vessels. They estimate that 800 000 kg of ash would have been used in only one year of ceramic production in the area surrounding Tikal (Ford and Glicken 1987:492). In light of this proposed high volume it is evident that any local source or sources of ash would necessarily need to be extensive and robust.

Ford and Rose (1995) propose that El Chichón, prime among the 16 volcanoes considered, might be a candidate for the origin of volcanic ash found in pottery. Ford and Rose consider the eruption history of El Chichón, located in Chiapas, Mexico, and suggest that favourable prevailing winds might have carried volcanic ash to the Belize River Valley region where potters incorporated the ash into ceramics in the Late Classic period. At the time of their paper, detailed tephrachronological studies had not been conducted on the El Chichón volcano; however, geologists Espíndola et al. (2000) have recently investigated its history. El Chichón is found approximately 50 miles south of modern Villahermosa and 80 km west of the site of Palenque (see Figure 6.6). The investigators were spurred to examine El Chichón due to its eruption in 1982 that caused serious devastation in nearby communities and an ash fall that affected a larger region in the eastern shadow of the volcano (Weintraub 1982). Isopach data

Figure 6.5 Thin Section Micrograph: Clear Glassy Shards of Volcanic AshUnder Plain Polarized Light

that outline the extent of the ensuing ash fall in 1982 reveal that El Chichón did not have ash fall in any direct proximity to the Belize River Valley. The furthest extent of ash fall from the 1982 eruption barely reached the northwestern most corner of Guatemala, well removed from the Belize Valley region. Although the eruption history of El Chichón coincides with archaeological chronology, logging eruptions during 553-614 A.D. and 676-788 A.D. (Espíndola, Marcías and Tilling 2000:102), it is unlikely that ash from these events reached the Belize Valley to find its way into ancient Maya ceramics.

Despite mounting evidence to the contrary, a local origin for volcanic ash wares continues to dominate current thinking. LeCount (1999) accepts the local ash source hypothesis for Xunantunich polychromes. She acknowledges the lack of local evidence of an ash source

as problematic, but continues to suggest this deficiency indicates that local ash sources were limited. Scarce local ash resources are used to support LeCount's theory that this added value to volcanic ash wares on the grounds of greater procurement costs involved in manufacture (LeCount 1999:248).

Arguments for local ash sources based on negative evidence are necessarily questionable, especially in light of the failure to identify sources in a number of studies seeking to address this specific issue. Given that geological and archaeological sourcing in the lowland region, including the Belize Valley, has not found suitable volcanic ash deposits in any significant quantity, alternate hypotheses need to be considered to explain the presence of volcanic ash petrofabrics in this region.

Hypothesis Two – Trade of Volcanic Ash

The second hypothesis suggests that volcanic ash was imported into the Belize Valley region and then incorporated into locally made ceramics. This second explanation for the presence of volcanic ash acknowledges that ash is not local to the Belize River Valley region; additionally, this theory operates under the assumption that volcanic petrofabrics are of local manufacture. Willey et al. (1965:371, 373) suggested Late Classic Belize Valley vessels with volcanic ash were made locally, based on the sheer ubiquity of ash wares at all the sites they surveyed in the region. The idea of local manufacture has endured since Willey et al.'s early statement and has virtually come to be accepted as common wisdom further reinforced by Gifford's (1976:255) naming of volcanic ash bearing ceramics at the Belize Valley site of Barton Ramie as "British Honduras Volcanic Ash Ware."

The "Volcanic 2" petrofabric is distinguished from "Volcanic 1" on the presence of crystalline calcite amounting to 1% to 3% of the fabric. The occurrence of calcite with volcanic ash suggests that there were at least two different sources of ash being used to manufacture vessels. Previously, Simmons and Brem (1979:83-85) have suggested that an extraregional source for volcanic ash, rather than trade of the actual vessels, was supported by their work in the northern Yucatan, Mexico. They found that Puuc Slate ware at Dzibilchaltun and Uxmal contained the ash in association with calcite and grog (sherd temper) inclusions. The presence of calcite with volcanic ash does not necessarily imply local production as Simmons and Brem have argued. Areas with volcanic activity may also have local limestone strata. A prime example of this would be the already much discussed El Chichón volcano in Chiapas, Mexico (Tilling 1982:673).

If we take Ford and Rose's suggestion that volcanic ash from El Chichón, Chiapas, is consistent with ash found in Belize Valley ceramics, I have calculated that volcanic ash mined at these sources would have had to have been transported over 475 km excluding geographic features, in a direct line as the crow flies, southwards. Other volcanoes considered as possible ash sources by Ford and Rose (1995:156) are equally distant. These distances are far outside of Arnold's (1981:36, 1985) optimal procurement zone for temper materials, usually less than eight kilometres and certainly not more than a day's travel away from the production locality. Ethnoarchaeological studies combined with petrographic analyses such as those of Druc (1996) in the Department of Ancash, Peru, have consistently backed Arnold's assertion that potters have a circumscribed area of procurement for production materials casting further doubt on the importation hypothesis.

Hypothesis Three – Trade of Volcanic Ash Ceramics

The occurrence of volcanic ash in ancient Maya ceramics is widespread throughout both the lowland and highland regions of the Maya area (see Figure 6.6). The Belize River Valley region and the northern Yucatan are certainly not isolated spots where volcanic ash petrofabrics are found. Jones (1986:45) reports ash wares at Tikal, Uaxactun, Altar de Sacrificios, Lubaantun, Rio Frio Cave "E," and San Jose. Simmons and Brem (1979) add Uxmal, Dzbilchaltun and Chichen Itza to this list. Rands (1967:142) has observed volcanic ash and pumice fragments in Palenque pottery. Volcanic ash ceramics have also been found in the Petexbatun region including the site of Dos Pilas in Guatemala by Foias and Bishop (1997:283) and Kepecs' (1998:126) work adds the Chikinchel region of the northeastern Yucatan to the growing roster of sites. Recently, Neff et al. (1999) have identified volcanic ash pottery at a number of southeastern Mesoamerican sites as well as El Mirador and Cuello (see Figure 6.6 Distribution of Sites with Volcanic Ash Ceramics).

Trade of pottery containing volcanic ash temper has been studied by archaeologists working outside of the Belize Valley area. Foias and Bishop (1997) have identified a small sample of monochrome and polychrome wares from the Petexbatún region, around the site of Dos Pilas, Guatemala, as containing volcanic ash. They have suggested that sources for the polychrome ceramics are in the upper middle Usumacinta and the Central Petén. Foias and Bishop (1997:283) classify the presence of volcanic ash polychromes as evidence of interregional exchange, linking the Petexbatun with regions such as the Usumacinta drainage area.

Rands (1967:142) questions where volcanic ash would have come from in ceramics at Palenque and other centres in the Usumacinta River region that are ostensibly alluvial sites. The extent of the 1982 ash fall due to the eruption of El Chichón may provide an answer. Where the Belize Valley region would have been beyond the reach of El Chichón's ash fall, sites such as Palenque in the Usumacinta region would lie directly beneath its shadow. In fact, photographs taken of Palenque after the 1982 eruption show its plaza areas covered in ash, as the site falls within the 20 mm deep area of the ash fall isopach (National Geographic Society 1982). Already mentioned in the discussion of hypothesis one, tephrachronological studies have demonstrated that eruptions of El Chichón did occur during periods when the ancient Maya would have occupied sites in the Usumacinta area. For sites such as Palenque, ash could have been a local resource for potters and, as demonstrated by Foias and Bishop (1997:283), such ceramics have found their way to other regions such as the Petexbatun.

Neff et al. (1999) have examined cream paste ceramics found in western El Salvador, northern Honduras and southern Guatemala. These cream paste wares were all found to contain volcanic ash inclusions. Compositional analyses, neutron activation and scanning electron microscopy were performed on pottery from a variety of sites in the above-mentioned regions. Neff et al. demonstrate that the source zone for the ceramics previously attributed to southern Guatemala and northern Honduras was actually western El Salvador suggesting interregional trade of these wares. Their analyses trace ceramics from the Late Formative to Late Classic periods establishing that widespread distribution of ceramics were long part of ancient Maya economic networks. Although of limited sample size, a number of Usulutan ceramics excavated at El Mirador (Petén) and Cuello (northern Belize) were tested in Neff et al.'s study. Usulutan ceramics (dating to the Formative and Early Classic periods) indicated that these sites, much removed from western El Salvador, were included in a far reaching distribution sphere.

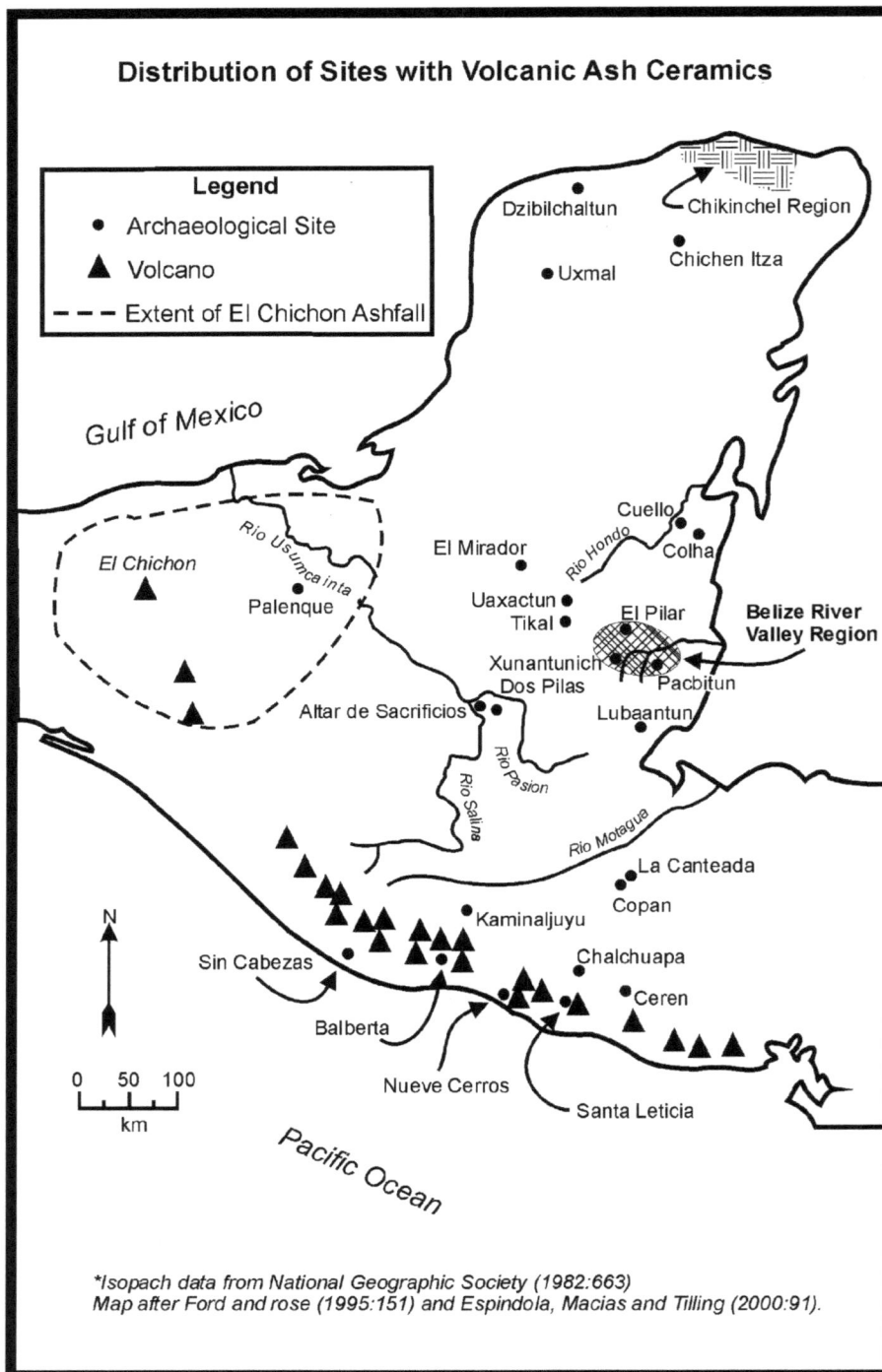

Figure 6.6 Distribution of Sites with Volcanic Ash Ceramics

Extraregional Petrofabrics – A Summation

In reviewing the evidence for the three hypotheses for volcanic ash petrofabrics in my Belize River Valley sample, I suggest that trade of finished vessels, rather than local production, is the most plausible theory. The first two theories, previously outlined, involving the local production of volcanic ash ceramics are not compelling especially given the lack of volcanic within the study region (hypothesis one) and the unlikely logistical conditions of trade in raw volcanic ash (hypothesis two). If Cuello participated in the distribution sphere of Formative period volcanic cream paste ceramics, (as discussed in hypothesis three) certainly the Belize Valley in the Late Classic period could have continued to interact with regions to the south in order to obtain ceramics. In fact, preliminary studies I have done on thin sections from Formative period Cahal Pech confirm the prescence of volcanic ash in select petrofabrics of this early period. (Formative period thin sections from Cahal Pech were not included in my present study.) Although the trade hypothesis goes against currently popular theories for the Belize Valley and other regions, an increasing number of studies (Neff et al., 1999) indicate that the extent and quantity of ceramic trade has been largely underestimated in Maya archaeology. I suggest that finished volcanic ash petrofabric ceramics were traded on a large, interregional scale.

The Belize River Valley – Scale and Integration of Economies

The general uniformity of petrofabric types for ceramics across the sites sampled in my study reflect a complex economy of regional proportions with significant interregional trade in volcanic ash wares. The ceramic economy was well integrated in the sense that assemblages at different sites were similar petrographically. Each of the eight sites in my sample had the same core suite of petrofabrics: "Calcite 1", "Calcite 2" and "Volcanic 1."

Extraregional ceramics represented by the "Volcanic 1" petrofabric were found at all sites, large and small, in this study. However, this is not to suggest that each centre would have directly imported these extraregional wares. A clue to a possible model describing the distribution of extraregional ceramics is observed through a consideration of the "Volcanic 2" petrofabric. "Volcanic 2" is found at a limited number of sites: Xunantunich, Pacbitun, El Pilar, Baking Pot and Ontario Village. It is significant that among these sites, Xunantunich displays the highest percentage of "Volcanic 2" at 14%. At this point, it is important to consider the archaeological context and history of the centre.

Leventhal et al., (1992:10) argue that the scale of hierarchical development for the Belize Valley region, as compared to that of the rest of the Maya lowlands, was decentralized until developments in the Late Classic

period when large centres such as Xunantunich, El Pilar, and Buenavista del Cayo emerged. During the Late Classic, Leventhal et al. (1992:11) see "…an increase in the localized concentration of authority within the region" and changes in political and economic structures. Ball and Taschek (1991) proposed that Xunantunich and Buenavista del Cayo were competing centres at the same hierarchical level during the Late Classic period. Leventhal et al. (1992:11-12) posit that Xunantunich replaced Buenavista del Cayo as the pre-eminent centre in the region. Ball and Taschek (1991) and Leventhal et al. (1992) all agree that the Belize River Valley region was tied and subordinate to the centre of Naranjo located in Guatemala based on comparison of epigraphic evidence from these sites.

Although samples were not obtained from Buenavista del Cayo for this study, it is of some import that of the sites included in the sample, Xunantunich was the one site during the Late Classic period that has concrete evidence of extraregional contact on a political level. It is plausible that political interactions were not the only modes of contact Xunantunich fostered on an extraregional scale. The economic importance and associated prestige of maintaining and funneling the flow of ceramics (specifically, volcanic ash ceramics that are slipped and some polychromes) into the valley region could certainly have spurred the political wrangling described between Xunantunich and Buenavista del Cayo.

The degree of integration did differ depending on the scale of the site itself. At this juncture a consideration of scale is most important in elucidating the nature of economic organization. The smaller sites of Floral Park and Blackman Eddy exhibited fewer petrofabric types than larger sites such as El Pilar and Xunantunich where the greatest variety of petrofabric types occurs. It is posited here that an intraregional distribution system was in operation. This intraregional system would have involved sites such as Xunantunich and El Pilar that redistributed extraregional imports throughout other sites in the region. At the same time, Xunantunich and El Pilar might have constituted a market for locally made ceramics thereby attracting pottery, such as "Granite 1" petrofabric vessels, made at other sites within its distribution sphere.

A Consideration of Models

The "inward-looking" and "outward-looking" economic models proposed by Rands (1967) and Rands and Bishop (1980) appear to be too constraining to directly apply to the Belize Valley data. It could be said that the distribution of the locally made "Granite 1" petrofabric would conform to the "inward-looking" model by using local resources and having a circumscribed distribution. However, the sole application of the "inward-looking" model would not be able to account for the regular provisioning of extraregional volcanic petrofabrics that would have to be described as typical of the "outward-looking" model. This study has shown that both "inward-" and "outward-looking" models can be applied to different portions of the ceramic economy for the Belize Valley material, but neither can account for the whole economic system.

Considering models of economic organization previously discussed in Chapter Two, the evidence presented here is most consistent with Fry's (1979:497) description of a complex market system. There is extensive distribution of calcite petrofabric types. Included in this widespread distributional patterning is the "Volcanic 1" petrofabric that also provides evidence of extraregional connections. Ceramic assemblages at politically important sites such as Xunantunich and El Pilar exhibit the greatest variety of petrofabric types. Geographically peripheral sites such as Floral Park and Blackman Eddy show a lesser degree of variation with a limited number of petrofabrics. Interpretation of the distributional patterning and variability of petrofabrics at the sites investigated allows for the formation of a tentative hierarchy of sites for the Late Classic period (see Figure 6.7).

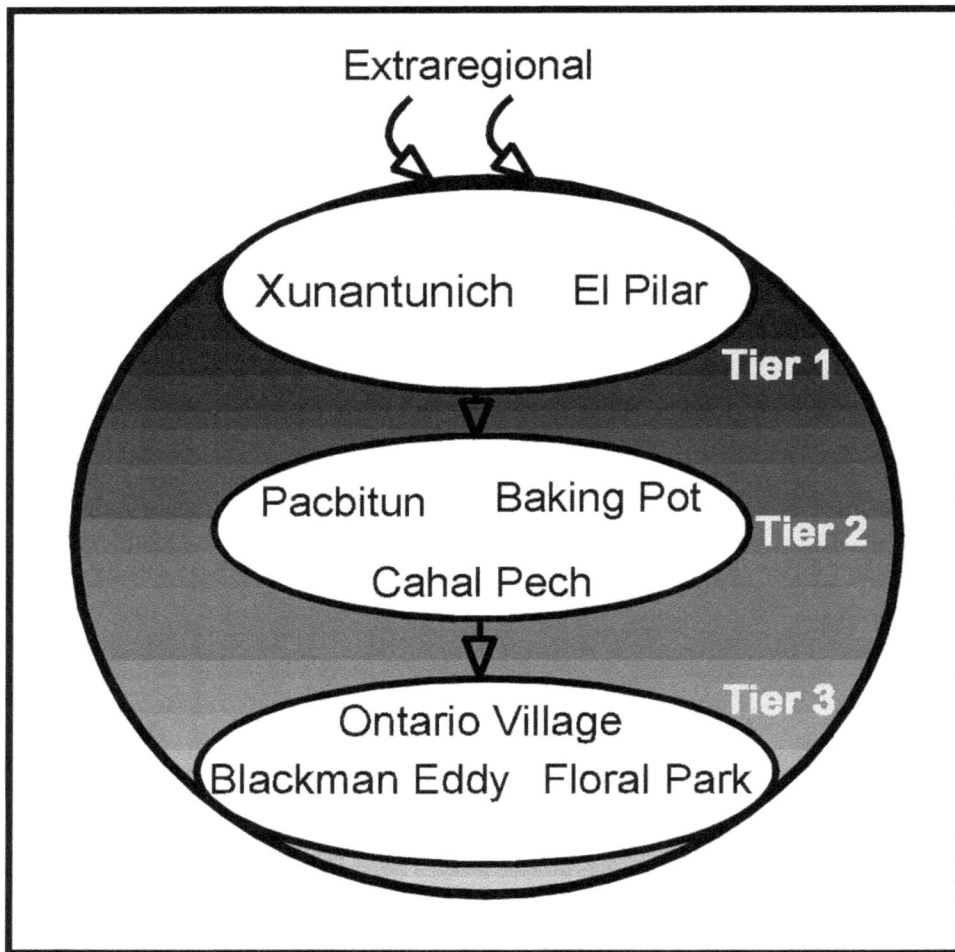

Figure 6.7 Tentative Site Hierarchy for Sites in this Study

7

Conclusions

Project Synopsis

The goal of this research was to investigate the nature and integration of ancient Maya economies through an examination of ceramic materials using petrographic and contextual analyses. In order to address issues concerning ceramic economy, a regional perspective was acknowledged as essential. The economic focus of this study necessitated including an array of sites varying in scale and complexity. Examining a single site would not adequately address the demands of investigating economic structures. The Belize River Valley region provided a suitable opportunity to examine a number of contemporaneous sites with provenanced ceramic assemblages. The eight sites that were included in this study were: Pacbitun, Xunantunich, El Pilar, Cahal Pech, Baking Pot Blackman Eddy, Floral Park and Ontario Village.

Ceramic petrology was used to characterize petrofabrics. Five petrofabrics were defined in this study: "Volcanic 1", "Volcanic 2", "Calcite 1", "Calcite 2" and "Granite 1." The subsequent tracing of the distributional patterning of petrofabrics enabled spheres of intersite economic interaction to be outlined. These interactions were proposed based on presence, absence and relative percentage of total ceramic assemblages at each of the sites when compared. Local petrofabric distributional patterns and their significance in local economic processes were explored.

Regional Interaction: Local Sources, Local Distribution Spheres

The data suggest that one important aspect of the Belize River Valley ceramic economy was the production of most utilitarian pottery on a local basis within the region. The calcite petrofabrics that comprised the great majority of utilitarian wares found at the eight sites were found to be consistent with the geological make-up of the region. "Calcite 1" petrofabric was represented by serving type vessels such as monochrome slipped bowls and dishes. "Calcite 2" petrofabric was found in the coarse unslipped vessel types including storage and cooking jars as well as larger bowls. All sites sampled included both calcite petrofabrics. The calcite petrofabrics can be considered of "local" origin, thereby representing regional ceramic production.

The "Granite 1" petrofabric was also found to be consistent with locally available resources. This petrofabric was represented by the same cooking and storage type vessels as that of "Calcite 2." Granitic sand taken from along the banks of the Belize River has the same mineral composition. "Granite 1" exhibited a restricted distribution being found in high frequency at sites such as Baking Pot and Pacbitun that would have had easy access to this raw material resource. Sites such as Xunantunich and El Pilar that may have acted as market or redistribution centres had more limited quantities of "Granite 1." Smaller sites and sites more distant from the resource as well as possible distribution centres, such as Floral Park, Blackman Eddy and Ontario Village did not include "Granite 1" in their assemblages thus delimiting a certain distribution sphere and a smaller role in the ceramic economy of the region.

Within the Belize River Valley region at least two different distributional patterns existed in the Late Classic for local petrofabrics. One sphere was defined by the uniform distribution of calcite petrofabrics that were present at every site in the study. A second, more exclusive sphere was marked by the distribution of the granite petrofabric. Through a consideration of these local petrofabrics it is possible to suggest that participation in distribution spheres for sites in the Belize Valley differed depending on their scale, complexity and access to resources.

Interregional Interaction: The Role of Extralocal Petrofabrics in Belize River Valley Ceramic Economy

The presence of ash-based petrofabrics, however, does suggest that these communities were involved in a wider sphere of economic exchange at some scale. After an examination of three different hypotheses for the presence of volcanic ash in Belize Valley ceramics, I propose that the volcanic petrofabrics were extraregional imports. Petrographic and contextual evidence best supports an outside source for these petrofabrics as formed vessels rather than the importation of raw ash to the valley region or the local sourcing of the volcanic ash. Importation of raw ash is unlikely since the very long travel distances to ash sources that would be necessary are not supported by ethnological and ethnoarchaeological studies. All attempts, including mine, to find local ash sources that match the volcanic ash identified in Belize River Valley ceramics have not been successful.

Additionally, it has been suggested that two or more sources of volcanic petrofabrics are likely. This theory was proposed based on the definition of two distinct petrofabrics, "Volcanic Ash 2" as distinguished from "Volcanic Ash 1" on the presence of crystalline calcite fragments. Moreover, the two volcanic petrofabrics also differed in their distribution across the region. "Volcanic Ash 1" was found at all sites in the sample while the smaller sites of Blackman Eddy and Floral Park did not include "Volcanic Ash 2." It is significant that the "Granite 1" petrofabric was also missing from the same sites of Blackman Eddy and Floral Park, further supporting the theory that these smaller scale sites participated in both in intraregional and interregional ceramic economic systems in a more limited fashion.

Late Classic Maya Economy and the Belize River Valley

This study has endeavoured to make a contribution towards better understanding of Late Classic Maya economies. It is noteable that findings here are consistent with the existence of economic relations of a much larger magnitude and complexity than has been the traditional speculation. Sites in the Belize River Valley participated in economic spheres of different scales suggesting a very complex economy: intraregional, regional and extraregional.

The data imply the presence of regional markets or a type of redistributive system by which locally made pottery as well as extraregional imports circulated. It is significant, however, to note that smaller sites had more limited access to imported ceramics indicating that redistributive mechanisms also operated on a subregional scale. The economic system described here is much more complex than can be simply portrayed as "inward-" or "outward-looking." By considering the hierarchy of sites, I propose it can be understood that there existed a diversity of distributive networks or spheres signifying varying degrees of involvement on the part of a number of sites or communities.

Future Research

Further research, as lightly touched upon in previous chapters, could take many possible directions. To broaden the perspective of regional economy investigated in this study other sites such as Buenavista del Cayo and Minanha may be added to the data set. Buenavista del Cayo and Minanha are located in the eastern section of the valley region, near the present day Belize – Guatemala border, near the Mopan River branch of the Belize River system. Buenavista would be especially interesting as it was a possible rival to Xunantunich in the Late Classic period for political control of the region. My study was not able to include Buenavista del Cayo and Minanha since investigation of these sites had just begun

and access could not be gained to the limited ceramic materials excavated at the time of my field research.

This study has identified Xunantunich and El Pilar as major centres on the basis of their participation in all the defined petrofabric distribution spheres. Extending a petrographic study to include Buenavista and other additional sites would refine our understanding of regional economic ceramic distribution spheres. This would further clarify our understanding of the political dynamic for the Late Classic period in the Belize River Valley. Which centres were hubs of trade and what roles would they fulfill in the redistributive hierarchy?

In contrast to the extensive approach described above, a more intensive direction may also be taken in future research. This study concentrated on examining a number of sites in the region through a synchronic perspective. Using a diachronic approach, sites may be intensively studied to trace the development of economic patterns through time. What type of distributional patterning was in evidence prior to the development of a complex market economy? When and how did these changes occur? Addressing these questions would provide a valuable insight into the development of complex economic systems. For this type of investigation a site with significant time depth as demonstrated by a long and continuous stratigraphic sequence of secure context would be required. Cahal Pech could be a candidate for such a study with evidence of occupation from the Early Middle Formative period to the Terminal Late Classic period.

On a smaller scale, additional work may be focused on specific petrological issues such as the refinement of the definitions for the calcite petrofabrics. This would entail detailed geological work sampling and describing locally available limestone sources in the region to provide comparative information for the ceramic petrofabric data. Ideally, this study would involve a sedimentary geologist interested in researching regional limestone variation. Thus far, the calcite petrofabrics have been defined based largely on grain size distribution. If an additional geological raw material sourcing provides a selection of differentiated calcites it might be possible to discern these in the petrofabrics. Distributional patterning of these petrofabrics might allow for finer observations on redistributive mechanisms in the regional economy.

Looking to interregional investigations, more research needs to be conducted on the volcanic ash petrofabrics to support the suggestion made here that these petrofabrics in the Belize River Valley region were imported from elsewhere. To this end, electron microprobe analyses could be used to characterize the elemental composition of the volcanic ash. Similar to trace element studies performed on obsidian, the compositional studies on volcanic ash can lead to the identification of ash sources. Once sources for the ash are located it would be possible to narrow down the areal search for centres producing these volcanic petrofabrics and articulate the interregional avenues of trade and economic interaction. Similarly, microprobe analyses could also separately test the nature of the clay matrix. Characterization of the clay matrix might allow one to further differentiate types and would aid in the identification of production centres.

Additionally, analyses performed by my study can be extended to other regions of the ancient Maya area. Already researchers from sites in regions outside of the Belize River Valley, such as northern Belize and Guatemala, have expressed to me their interest in this type of research. Standardized application of the research methodology and analytical techniques I used would result in a uniform petrologically based typology that could be used to compare assemblages on at site-to-site and regional basis. The spread of this kind of research would aid greatly in the consolidation of information on Maya ceramics. It would also promote comparative research by providing a concrete foundation for the assessment of economic systems.

As has been demonstrated, the more that has been discovered, the more there is to be learned. Certainly, this comment is an often repeated maxim, but it is never more applicable than in our ongoing attempts to understand complex human systems such as economies. Research in such multifaceted issues provides the archaeological discipline with a significant challenge, especially given the limited array of material evidence available. This places the onus on researchers to demand more of their data sets, being aware of the wide spectrum of possible implications, whether it is concentrating on intricate details or employing broader perspectives.

REFERENCES

Aimers, J.J.
    1997 Preliminary Investigations of Architecture in Plaza 2 of Group 1 at Baking Pot, Belize. In *Belize Valley Archaeological Reconnaissance Project: Progress Report of the 1997 Field Season*. J.J. Awe ed., pp. 21-46. Ms. On file, Department of Archaeology, Belmopan, Belize.

Angelini, M.L.
    1998 *The Potter's Craft: A Study of Formative Maya Ceramic Technology at K'axob Belize*. Unpublished Ph.D. Dissertation. Department of Anthropology, Boston University, Boston.

Arnold D.E.
    1971 Ethnomineralogy of Ticul, Yucatan, potters: Etics and emics. *American Antiquity* 36(1):20-240.
    1972 Mineralogical Analyses of Ceramic Materials from Quinua, Department of Ayacucho, Peru. *Archaeometry* 14(1):93-102.
    1975 Ceramic Ecology of the Ayacucho Basin, Peru: Implications for Prehistory. *Current Anthropology* 16(2):183-206.
    1978 Ethnography of pottery-making in the Valley of Guatemala. In *The Ceramics of Kaminaljuyu, Guatemala*. ed, R.K. Wetherington, pp. 327-400. Pennsylvania State University Press, University Park.
    1985 *Ceramic Theory and Cultural Process*. Cambridge University Press, Cambridge.

Arnold, P.J.
    1991 *Domestic Ceramic Production and Spatial Organization: A Mexican Case Study in Ethnoarchaeology*. University of Cambridge, Cambridge.

Ashmore, W.
    1995 Settlement Archaeology at Xunantunich, 1995. In *Xunantunich Archaeological Project 1995 Field Season Report*. R.M. Leventhal (ed.) pp. 10-25. MS on file Department of Archaeology, Belize, Central America.

Awe, J.J.
    1992 *Dawn in the Land Between the Two Rivers: Formative Occupation at Cahal Pech, Belize and its Implication to Preclassic Maya Development in the Central Maya Lowlands*. Ph.D. diss., University of London.

    1993 *Belize Valley Archaeological Reconnaissance Project: Progress Report of the 1992 Field Season*. Ms., Trent University, Peterborough, Ontario.

Awe, J.J., C.G.B. Helmke and C.S. Griffith
    1998 Archaeological Reconnaissance in the Roaring Creek Valley: Caves, Rockshelters, and Settlement Architecture. In The Western Belize Regional Cave Project Report of 1997 Field Investigations. J.J. Awe (ed.) pp. 216-229. MS on file Department of Archaeology, Belize, Central America.

Awe, J.J., and M. Campbell
    1988 *Site Core Investigations at Cahal Pech, Cayo District, Belize: Preliminary Report of the 1988 Season*. Trent University, Peterborough, Ontario.

Ball, J.W.
    1976 Ceramic Sphere Affiliations of the Barton Ramie Ceramic Complexes. In *Prehistoric Pottery Analysis and the Ceramics of Barton Ramie in the Belize Valley*. J.C. Gifford, ed., pp. 323-330. Memoirs of the Peabody Museum of Archaeology and Ethnology, Volume 18. Harvard University, Cambridge.
    1993 Pottery, Potters, Palaces, and Polities: Some Socioeconomic and Political Implications of Late Classic Maya Ceramic Industries. In *Lowland Maya Civilization in the Eighth Century A.D.: a Symposium at Dumbarton Oaks, 7th and 9th October 1989*. J.A. Sabloff and J.S. Henderson eds., pp. 243-272. Dumbarton Oaks Trustees for Harvard University, Washington, D.C.

Ball, J.W., and J.T. Taschek
    1991 Late Classic Lowland Maya Political Organization and Central Place Analysis: New Insights from the Upper Belize Valley. *Ancient Mesoamerica* 2(2):149-166.

Beaudry, M.P.
    1987 Southeast Maya Polychrome Pottery: Production, Distribution and Style. In *Maya Ceramics: Papers from the 1985 Maya Ceramic Conference*. P.M. Rice and R.J. Sharer eds., pp. 503-523. BAR International Series 345 (ii), Oxford.

Blanton, R.E.
1983 Factors Underlying the Origin and Evolution of Market Systems, In *Economic Anthropology.* Monographs in Economic Anthropology: No. 1., S. Ortiz, ed., University Press of America, Boston.

Blanton, R. E., S.A. Kowalewski, G.M. Feinman, and L. M. Finsten
1993 *Ancient Mesoamerica: A Comparison of Change in Three Regions.* Cambridge University Press, Cambridge.

Bonis, S., and O.H. Bohnenberger
1970 *Mapa Geológico de la República de Guatemala 1970.* Instituto Geográfico Nacional, Guatemala City.

Bullard, W.R. Jr. and M. Ricketson Bullard
1965 *Late Classic Finds at Baking Pot, British Honduras.* Art and Archaeology Occasional Paper 8., Royal Ontario Museum and the University of Toronto, Toronto.

Chase, A.F.
1992 Elites and the Changing Organization of Classic Maya Society. In *Mesoamerican Elites: An Archaeological Assessment.* D.Z. Chase and A.F. Chase (eds.), pp. 30-49. University of Oklahoma Press, Norman.

Conlon, J.M. and J.J. Ehret
1999 Ancient Maya Settlement at Baking Pot, Belize: Results of the Continually Expanding Survey Program in the Search for the End of the Final Frontier. *Belize Valley Archaeological Reconnaissance Project: Progress Report of the 1999 Field Season.* Ms. On file with author.

Costin, C.L.
1991 Craft Specialization: Issues in Defining, Documenting, and Explaining the Organization of Production. *Archaeological Method and Theory* vol. 3., M.B. Schiffer (ed.), pp.1-56. University of Arizona Press, Tucson.

Costin, C.L., and T. Earle
1989 Status Distinction and Legitimation of Power as Reflected in Changing Patterns of Consumption in Late Prehispanic Peru. *American Antiquity* 54(4):691-714.

Cowgill, G.L.
1992 Social Differentiation at Teotihuacan. In *Mesoamerican Elites: An Archaeological Assessment.* D.Z. Chase and A.F. Chase eds., pp. 206-220. University of Oklahoma Press, Norman.

Culbert, T. P.
1977 Maya Development and Collapse: An Economic Perspective. In *Social Processes and Maya Prehistory.* Pp. 510-530. Norman Hammond, ed. Academic Press, London.

Curet, A.
1993 Regional Studies and Ceramic Production Areas: An Example from La Mixtequilla, Veracruz, Mexico. *Journal of Field Archaeology* 20:427-440.

De Atley, S.P., and R.L. Bishop
1991 Toward and Integrated Interface for Archaeology and Archaeometry. In *The Ceramic Legacy of Anna O. Sheppard.* R.L. Bishop and F.W. Lange, eds., pp. 358-380. University Press of Colorado, Niwot, Colorado.

Dreiss, M.L., D.O. Brown, T.R. Hester, M.D. Glascock, H. Neff, K.S. Stryker.
1993 Expanding the Role of Trace-Element Studies: Obsidian Use in the Late and Terminal Classic Periods at the Lowland Maya Site of Colha, Belize. *Ancient Mesoamerica.* 4(2):271-283.

Driver, W.D., and J.K. McWilliams
1995 Excavations at the Ontario Village Site. In *The Belize Valley Archaeology Project: Results of the 1994 Field Season.* J.F. Garber ed., pp. 26-57. Ms. Department of Anthropology, Southwest Texas State University, San Marcos.

Druc, I.C.
1996 De la Etnografía hacia la Arquelogía: Aportes de Entrvistas con Ceramistas de Ancash (Péru) para la Caracterización de la Cerámica Prehispánica. *Bulletin for the Institute of Andean Studies* 25(1):17-41.

Ehert, J.J.
1995 The Xunantunich Settlement Survey Test-Pittting Program. In *Xunantunich Archaeological Project 1995 Field Season Report,* R.M. Leventhal, ed. pp. 164-192. MS on file Department of Archaeology, Belize, Central America.

Espínola, J.M., J.L. Macías, R.I. Tilling, and M.F. Sheridan
2000 Volcanic History of El Chichón Volcano (Chiapas, Mexico) During the Holocene, and its Impact on Human Activity. *Bulletin of Volcanology* 62:90-104.

Fedick, S.L.
1988 *Prehistoric Maya Settlement and Land Use Patterns in the Upper Belize River Area, Belize, Central America.* Unpublished Ph.D. Dissertation, Arizona State University.
1989 The Economics of Agricultural Land Use and Settlement in the Upper Belize River Valley. In *Research in Economic Anthropology, Supplement 4*, P. McAnany and B. Isaac, eds., pp. 215-253.

Foias, A.E., and R.L. Bishop
1997 Changing Ceramic Production and Exchange in the Petexbatun Region, Guatemala:

Reconsidering the Classic Maya Collapse. *Ancient Mesoamerica* 8(2): 2275-292.

Folk, R. L.
1980 *Petrology of Sedimentary Rocks.* Austin, Hemphill.

Ford, A.
1990 Settlement and Environment in the Upper Belize River Area and Variability in Household Organization. In *Prehistoric Population History in the Maya Lowlands,* T.P. Culbert and D.S. Rice, eds., pp. 167-182. University of New Mexico Press, Albuquerque.
1991 Economic Variation of Ancient Maya Residential Settlement in the Upper Belize River Area. *Ancient Mesoamerica* 2:35-46.

Ford, A., and S.L. Fedick
1992 Prehistoric Maya Settlement Patterns in the Upper Belize River Area: Initial Results of the Belize River Archaeological Settlement Survey. *Journal of Field Archaeology* 19:35-49.

Ford, A. and H. Glicken
1987 The Significance of Volcanic Ash Tempering in the Ceramics of the Central Maya Lowlands. In *Maya Ceramics: Papers from the 1985 Maya Ceramic Conference.* P.M. Rice and R.J. Sharer eds., pp. 479-502. BAR International Series 345 (ii), Oxford.

Ford, A., W. I. Rose
1995 Volcanic Ash in Ancient Maya Ceramics of the Limestone Lowlands: Implications for Prehistoric Volcanic Activity in the Guatemalan Highlands. *Journal of Volcanology and Geothermal Research* 66:149-162.

Ford, A. and D.C. Wernecke
1996 *The Trails of El Pilar: A Guide to the El Pilar Archaeological Reserve for Maya Flora and Fauna.* CORI Mesoamerican Research Center, University of Calafornia, Santa Barbara.

Friedel, D.A.
1978 Maritime Adaptation and the Rise of Maya Civilization: The View from Cerros, Belize. In *Prehistoric Coastal Adaptations.* B. Stark and B. Voorhies eds., pp. 239-265. Academic Press, New York.

Freestone, I.C.
1991 Extending Ceramic Petrology. In *Recent Developments in Ceramic Petrology.* A.P. Middleton and I.C. Freestone, eds., pp. 399-410. British Museum Occasional Paper No. 81., British Museum, London.
1995 Ceramic Petrology. *Journal of Field Archaeology* 99:111-115.

Freestone, I.C., C. Johns, and T. Potter, eds.
1982 *Current Research in Ceramics: Thin-section Studies.* British Museum Occasional Papers No. 32, Trustees of the British Museum, London.

Fry, R.E.
1979 The Economics of Pottery at Tikal, Guatemala: Models of Exchange for Serving Vessels. *American Antiquity* 44(3):494-512.
1980 Models of Exchange for Major Shape Classes of Lowland Maya Pottery. In *Models and Methods in Regional Exchange.* R.E. Fry ed., SAA Papers 1:3-18.

Garber, J.F., K.M. Brown, and C.J. Hartman
1998 Middle Preclassic Public Architecture: The Blackman Eddy Example. In *The Belize Valley Archaeology Project: Results of the 1997 Field Season.* J.F. Garber ed., pp. 5-32. Ms. Department of Anthropology, Southwest Texas State University, San Marcos.

Garber, J.F., D.M. Glassman, W.D. Driver, and P. Weiss
1994 *The Belize Valley Archaeology Project: Results of the 1993 Field Season.* Ms. Department of Anthropology, Southwest Texas State University, San Marcos.

Garber, J.F., Reilly, K., and D.M. Glassman
1995 Excavations on Structure B1 at Blackman Eddy. In *The Belize Valley Archaeology Project: Results of the 1994 Field Season.* J.F. Garber ed., pp. 4-20. Ms. Department of Anthropology, Southwest Texas State University, San Marcos.

Gibson, E.C.
1986 *Diachronic Patterns of Lithic Production, Use, and Exchange in the Southern Maya Lowlands.* Unpublished Ph.D. Dissertation, Department of Anthropology, Harvard University, Cambridge.

Gifford, J.C.
1960 The Type-variety Method of Ceramic Classification as an Indicator of Cultural Phenomena. *American Antiquity* 25(3):341-354.
1976 *Prehistoric Pottery Analysis and the Ceramics of Barton Ramie in the Belize Valley.* Memoirs of the Peabody Museum of Archaeology and Ethnology, Volume 18. Harvard University, Cambridge.

Glassman, D. M., J.M. Conlon, and J. F. Garber
1995 Survey and Initial Excavations at Floral Park. In *The Belize Valley Archaeological Project: Results of the 1994 Field Season.* Eds. J.F. Garber and D.M. Glassman. Pp. 58-70. Southwest Texas State University, San Marcos.

Goldsmith, S.A.
1992 Report on the 1991 Excavations at the K'ik Group, Cahal Pech, Belize. In *Progress Report of the Fourth Field Season (1991) of Investigations at Cahal Pech, Belize.* J.J. Awe, ed., pp. 9-34.

Ms., Department of Archaeology, Trent University, Peterborough, Ontario.

1993 *Household Archaeology in theBelize River Valley: An Analysis of Current Issues.* Unpublished M.A. Thesis, Department of Archaeology, University of Calgary, Calgary, Alberta.

Graham, E.
1987 Resource Diversity in Belize and its Implications for Models of Lowland Trade. *American Antiquity*, 52(4):753-767.

Graham, E., L. McNatt., and M.A. Gutchen
1980 Excavations in Footprint Cave, Caves Branch, Belize. *Journal of Field Archaeology* 7:153-172.

Hammond, N.
1972 Obsidian Trade Routes in the Mayan Area. *Science.* 178:1092-1093.
1982 *Ancient Maya Civilization.* Rutgers University Press, New Brunswick.

Hammond, N., G. Harbottle, and T. Gazard.
1976 Neutron Activation and Statistical Analysis of Maya Ceramics and Clays From Lubaantun, Belize. *Archaeometry.* 18(2):147-168.

Hays, T.R. and F.A. Hassan
1974 Mineralogical Analysis of Sudanese Neolithic Ceramics. *Archaeometry* 16(1):71-79.

Healy, P.F.
1985 *Report on 1984 Test Excavations at Pacbitun (Site #28/189-30) Cayo District, Belize.* Ms. On file, Social Sciences and Humanities Research Council of Canada, Ottawa.
1990 Excavations at Pacbitun, Belize: Preliminary Report on the 1986 and 1987 Investigations. *Journal of Field Archaeology* 17:247-262.
1992 The Ancient Maya Ballcourt at Pacbitun, Belize. *Ancient Mesoamerica* 3(2):229-239.

Healy, P.F., J.J. Awe, and G. Iannone
1993 Pacbitun and Ancient Maya Slate Use. Paper presented at Society for American Archaeology 58th Annual Meeting, St. Louis, MI.

Iannone, G.
1993 "Time Among the Thorns: Results of the 1992 Field Season at Zubin, Cayo District, Belize." In *Belize Valley Archaeological Reconnaissance Project: Progress Report of the 1992 Field Season.* Jaime J. Awe ed., pp. 10-44. Trent University, Peterborough.

Iceland, H.B.
1999 Late-Terminal Classic Maya Pottery in Northern Belize: A Petrographic Analysis of Sherd Samples from Colha and Kichpanha. *Journal of Archaeological Science* 26:951-966.

Isaac, B.L.
1996 Approaches to Classic Maya Economies. *Reseach in Economic Anthropology* 17:297-334.

Jones, L.D.
1986 *Lowland Maya Pottery: The Place of Petrological Analysis.* BAR International Series 288, Oxford.

Kaiser, T.
1989 Steatite-Tempered Pottery from Selevac, Yugoslavia: A Neolithic Experiment in Ceramic Design. *Archaeomaterials* 3:1-10.

Kamilli, D.C., C.C. Lamberg-Karlovsky
1979 Petrographic and Electron Microprobe Analysis of Ceramics from Tepe Yahya, Iran. *Archaeometry* 36(1):47-59.

Keller, Angie, H.
1993 Vision and Revision: The Remapping of Xunantunich. In *Xunantunich Archaeological Project: 1993 Field Season.* R.M. Leventhal, ed., pp. 87-99. Ms. On file, Belize Department of Archaeology, Belmopan, Belize.

Kosakowsky, L.J.
1987 *Preclassic Maya Pottery at Cuello, Belize.* Anthropological Papers of the University of Arizona, number 47, University of Arizona Press, Tuscon.

La Lone, D.E.
1994 An Andean World-System: Production Transformations Under the Inka Empire. In *The Economic Anthropology of the State.* Monographs in Economic Anthropology; No. 11., University Press of America, Landham, Maryland.

LeCount, L.J.
1999 Polychrome Pottery and Political Strategies in Late and Terminal Classic Lowland Maya Society. *Latin American Antiquity* 10(3):239-258.

Leventhal, R.M.
1992 Introduction. In *Xunantunich Archaeological Project: 1992 Field Season.* R.M. Leventhal, ed., pp. 1-7. Ms. On file, Belize Department of Archaeology, Belmopan, Belize.

Leventhal, R.M., W. Ashmore, L. LeCount, V. Hetrick, and T. Jamison
1992 Xunantunich Archaeological Project 1992 Research. Paper presented at the 91st Annual Meeting American Anthropological Association, San Francisco, CA.

Lucero, L.J.
1994 *Household and Community Integration among Hinterland Elites and Commoners: Maya Residential Ceramic Assemblages of the Belize River Area.* Unpublished Ph.D. dissertation,

Department of Anthropology, University of California, Los Angeles.

Mason, R.B.
1991 Petrology of Islamic Ceramics. In *Recent Developments in Ceramic Petrology.* A.P. Middleton and I.C. Freestone, eds., pp. 185-209. British Museum Occasional Paper No. 81., British Museum, London.
1994 *Islamic Glazed Pottery: 700-1250.* Unpublished Ph.D. Dissertation, Wolfson College, Oxford University.
2004 *Shine Like the Sun: Lustre-painted and Associated Pottery from the Medieval Middle East,* Mazda Press, Costa Mesa, California, and Royal Ontario Museum, Toronto

Mason, R.B., and L. Cooper
1999 Grog, Petrology and Early Transcaucasians at Godin Tepe. *Iran* XXXVII:25-33.

Mason, R.B., and E.J. Keall
1988 Provenance of Local Ceramic Industry and the Characterization of Imports: Petrography of Pottery from Medieval Yemen. *Antiquity* 62:452-463.

Mason, R.B., and M.S. Tite
1994 The Beginnings of Stone Paste Technology. *Archaeometry* 36(1):77-91.

McAnany, P.A.
1989a Introduction. In *Prehistoric Maya Economies of Belize.* Research in Economic Anthropology, A Research Annual. JAI Press, London.
1989b Economic Foundations of Prehistoric Maya Society: Paradigms and Concepts. In *Prehistoric Maya Economies of Belize.* Research in Economic Anthropology, A Research Annual. JAI Press, London.
1989c Stone Tool Production and Exchange in the Eastern Maya Lowlands: The Consumer Perspective from Pulltrouser Swamp, Belize. *American Antiquity* 54(2):332-346.
1991 Structure and Dynamics of Intercommunity Exchange. In *Maya Stone Tools: Selected Papers from the Second Maya Lithics Conference,* eds, Thomas R. Hester and Harry J. Iceland. Pp. 271-293. Monographs in World Archaeology No. 1. Prehistory Press, Madison.
1992 A Theoretical Perspective on Elites and the Economic Transformation of Classic Period Maya Households. In *Understanding Economic Process.* S. Ortiz, and S. Lees eds., pp. 85-103. Monographs in Economic Anthropology, No. 10. University Press of America, Landham, Maryland.

McKillop, H.
1996 Ancient Maya Trading Ports and the Integration of Long-Distance and Regional Economies. *Ancient Mesoamerica* 7:49-62.

McKillop, H., L. Jackson, H. Michel, F. Stross and F. Asaro
1988 Chemical Source Analysis of Maya Obsidian artifacts: New Perspectives From Wild Cane Cay, Belize. In *Archaeometry 88: Proceedings of the 1988 International Symposium on Archaeometry,* eds., R.M. Farquhar, R.G.V. Hancock, R. Farquar, and L. Pavlish. pp. 239-244. University of Toronto, Toronto.

Middleton, A.P., I.C. Freestone, and M.N. Leese.
1985 Textural Analysis of Ceramic Thin Sections: Evaluation of Grain Sampling Proceedures. *Archaeometry* 27(1):64-74.

Moholy-Nagy. H.
1983 The Flaked Chert Industry of Tikal, Guatemala. Paper presented at the Second Symposium on Lowland Maya Lithics, San Antonio, Texas.

Moore, A.F.
1997 Intragroup Comparative Study of the Ancient Maya in the Periphery of Baking Pot: Report on the First Season of Investigations at the Atalaya Group. In *Belize Valley Archaeological Reconnaissance Project: Progress Report of the 1997 Field Season.* J.J. Awe ed., pp. 47-58. Ms. On file, Belize Department of Archaeology, Belmopan, Belize.

Morris, E.L.
1991 Ceramic Analysis and the Pottery from Potterne: A Summary. In *Recent Developments in Ceramic Petrology.* A.P. Middleton and I.C. Freestone, eds., pp. 277-288. British Museum Occasional Paper No. 81, British Museum, London.

National Geographic Society
1982 The Disaster of El Chichon. *National Geographic* 162(5):654-684.

Neff, H., J.W. Cogswell, L.J. Kosakowsky, F. Estrada Belli, and F.J. Bove
1999 A New Perspective on the Relationships among Cream Paste Ceramic Traditions of Southeastern Mesoamerica. *Latin American Antiquity,* 10(3): 281-299.

Nelson, F.W., K.K. Nielson., N. Mangelson, M.W. Hill, R.T. Matheny
1977 Preliminary Studies of the Trace Element Composition of Obsidian Artifacts from Northern Campeche, Mexico. *American Antiquity* 42:209-224.

Orton, C., P. Tyers and A. Vince
1993 *Pottery in Archaeology.* Cambridge University Press, Cambridge.

Peacock, D.P.S.
1969 Neolithic Pottery Production in Cornwall. *Antiquity* 43:145-149.
1982 *Pottery in the Roman World.* Longman, London.

Pettijohn, F. J., P. E. Potter and R. Siever
1987 *Sand and Sandstone.* 2nd ed. New York and Berlin: Springer-Verlag.

Polanyi, K., C.M. Arensberg, and H.W. Pearson eds.
1957 *Trade and Markets in the Early Empires.* Free Press, Glencoe, IL.

Powis, T.
1993 Burning the Champa: Investigations at the Tolok Group, Cahal Pech, Belize. In *Belize Valley Archaeological Recconnaissance Project: Progress Report of the 1992 Field Season.* J.J. Awe ed., pp. 97-115. Ms., Trent University, Peterborough, Ontario.
1994 Sacred Space and Ancestor Worship: Ongoing Plaza Investigations of Two Middle Formative Circular Platforms art the Tolok Group, Cahal Pech, Belize. In *Belize Valley Archaeological Recconnaissance Project: Progress Report of the Sixth (1993) Field Season.* J.J. Awe ed., pp. 122-146. Ms. Institute of Archaeology, University of London, London.

Preece, S.
2001 Post Doctoral Fellow, University of Toronto, Department of Geology, Toronto.

Pring, D.C.
1980 *The Preclassic Ceramics of Northern Belize.* Ph.D. diss., University of London, University Microfilms International, Ann Arbor.

Rands, R.L.
1967 Ceramic Technology and Trade in the Palenque Region, Mexico. In *American Historical Anthropology.* C.L. Riley and W.W. Taylor eds., pp. 137-151. Southern Illinois Press, Carbondale and Edwardsville.

Rands, R.L., and R.L. Bishop
1980 Resource Procurement Zones and Patterns of Ceramic Exchange in the Palenque Region, Mexico. In *Models and Methods in Regional Exchange,* ed., R.E. Fry. pp. 19-46. SAA Papers No. 1.

Reese, K.V., and F. Valdez Jr.
1987 The Ceramic Sequence of Kichpanha: 1979-1985 Seasons. In *Maya Ceramics: Papers from the 1985 Maya Ceramic Conference* P.M. Rice., and R.J. Sharer., eds., pp. 37-46. International Series 345, B.A.R., Oxford.

Reina, R.E., and R.M. Hill, II
1978 *The Traditional Pottery of Guatemala.* University of Texas Press, Austin.

Rice, P.M.
1987a Economic Change in the Lowland Maya Late Classic. In *Specialization, Exchange, and Complex Societies.* E.M. Brumfiel and T.K. Earle, eds., pp. 76-85. Cambridge University Press, Cambridge.
1987b Lowland Maya Pottery Production in the Late Classic Period. In *Maya Ceramics: Papers from the 1985 Maya Ceramic Conference.* P.M. Rice and R.J. Sharer eds., pp. 525-543. BAR International Series 345 (ii), Oxford.
1987c *Pottery Technology: A Source Book.* University of Chicago Press, Chicago.

Ritchie, C.F.
1990 *Ancient Maya Settlement and Environment of the Eastern Zone of Pacbitun, Belize.* Unpublished M.A. Thesis, Department of Anthropology, Trent Univerisity, Peterborough, Ontario.

Renfrew, C.
1977 Alternative Models for Exchange and Spatial Distribution. Im, *Exchange Systems in Prehistory.* T.K. Earle and J.E. Ericson, eds., pp. 71-90. Academic Press, New York.

Sabloff, J.A.
1975 *Excavations at Seibal, Deapartment of Peten, Guatemala. Ceramics.* Memoirs of the Peabody Museum of Archaeology and Ethnology, vol.13, no.2. Harvard University, Cambridge.

Sabloff, J.A. and W.L. Rathje
1973 A Study of Changing Pre-Commercial Patterns on the Island of Cozumel, Mexico. *Proceedings of the 40th International Congress of Americanists* 1:455-463.
1975 The Rise of a Maya Merchant Class. *Scientific American* 233(4):72-82.

Santley, R.S., P.J. Arnold, III., and C.A. Pool
1989 The Ceramic Production System at Matacapan, Veracruz, Mexico. *Journal of Field Archaeology* 16:107-131.

Sattherwaite, L. Jr.
1951 Reconnaissance in British Honduras. *The University Museum Bulletin* 3216(1):21-36.

Shafer, H.J. and T.R. Hester
1983 Ancient Maya Chert Workshops in Northern Belize, Central America. *American Antiquity* 48:519-543.

Sheppard, A.O.
1939 Technological Notes on the Pottery of San Jose. Appendix B. In *Excavations at San Jose, British Honduras.* Ed., J. E. Thompson. Pp. 251-

277. Carnegie Institution of Washington, Washington D.C.
1956 *Ceramics for the Archaeologist.* Carnegie Institution of Washington, Washington, D.C.

Shipley, W.E. III
1978 *Geology, Petrology, and Geochemistry of the Mountain Pine Ridge Batholith, Belize, Central America.* Unpublished M.Sc. Thesis, Colorado School of Mines, Golden, CO.

Simmons, M.P., and G.F. Brem
1979 The Analysis and Distribution of Volcanic Ash-Tempered Pottery in the Lowland Maya Area. *American Antiquity* 44(1):79-91.

Sinopoli, C.M.
1991 *Approaches to Archaeological Ceramics.* Plenum Press, New York.

Spence, M.W.
1996 Commodity of Gift: Teotihuacan Obsidian in the Maya Region. *Latin American Antiquity* 7(1):21-39.

Stoltman, J.B.
1991 Ceramic Petrography as a Techniques for Documenting Cultural Interaction: An Example from the Upper Mississippi Valley. *American Antiquity* 56(1):103-120.

Sunahara, K.S.
1995 *Ancient Maya Settlement: The Western Zone of Pacbitun, Belize.* Unpublished M.A.Thesis, Department of Anthropology, Trent University, Peterborough, Ontario.

Terry, R.D., and G.V. Chillingar
1955 Summary of "Concerning Some Additional Aids in Studying Sedimentary Formations" by M.S. Shvestsov" *Journal of Sedimentary Petrology* 25:229-234.

Valdez, F., Jr.
1987 *The Prehistoric Ceramics of Colha, Northern Belize.* Unpublished Ph. D. Dissertation, Department of Anthropology, Harvard University, Cambridge.

Wardle, P.
1992 *Earlier Prehistoric Pottery Production and Ceramic Petrology in Britain.* B.A.R., Oxford.

Wattenmaker, P.
1993 Household Economy in Early State Society: Material Value, Productive Context and Spheres of Exchange. In *The Economic Anthropology of the State.* Monographs in Economic Anthropology, No. 11. University Press of America, Landham, Maryland.

Weintraub, B.
1982 Fire and Ash Darkness at Noon. *National Geographic* 162(5):660-684.

Williams, D.F.
1983 Petrology of Ceramics. In *The Petrology of Archaeological Artefacts.* D.R.C. Kempe and A.P. Harvey eds., pp. 301-329. Clarendon Press, Oxford.

Willey, G.R.
1973 Man, Settlement and Urbanism. *Antiquity* 47:269-279.

Willey, G.R., W.R. Bullard., J.B. Glass Jr., and J.C. Gifford
1965 *Prehistoric Settlements in the Belize Valley.* Papers of the Peabody Museum of Archaeology and Ethnology, vol. 54. Harvard University, Cambridge.

Willey, G.R., Culbert, T.P. and R.E.W. Adams
1967 Maya Lowland Ceramics: A Report from the 1965 Guatemala City Conference. *American Antiquity* 32(3):289-315.

Yaeger, J.
1992 Xunantunich Settlement Survey. In *Xunantunich Archaeological Project 1992 Field Season Report.* R.M. Leventhal (ed.) pp. 110-126. MS on file Department of Archaeology, Belize, Central America.

Appendix A

Inventory of Thin Sectioned Sherds from Cahal Pech by Petrofabric

PETROFABRIC	SHERD	CONTEXT	TYPE-VARIETY
CALCITE 1	CP - 54A	KIK GROUP STR 1 LVL 4 UNITS 1 & 9	BELIZE RED
CALCITE 1	CP - 24	PLAZA B LVL 1-2 UNIT 1	DOLPHIN HEAD RED
CALCITE 1	CP - 25	PLAZA B LVL 1-2 UNIT 1	DOLPHIN HEAD RED
CALCITE 1	CP - 58	KIK GROUP STR 1 LVL 4 UNITS 1 & 9	DOLPHIN HEAD RED
CALCITE 1	CP - 55B	KIK GROUP STR 1 LVL 4 UNITS 1 & 9	DOLPHIN HEAD RED
CALCITE 1	CP - 64	FIGUEROA GROUP STR 3 LVL 1-2 UNIT 1	DOLPHIN HEAD RED
CALCITE 1	CP - 65	FIGUEROA GROUP STR 3 LVL 1-2 UNIT 1	GARBUTT CREEK RED
CALCITE 1	CP - 26	PLAZA B LVL 1-2 UNIT 1	ROARING CREEK RED
CALCITE 2	CP - 23B	PLAZA B LVL 1-2 UNIT 1	ALEXANDERS UNSLIPPED
CALCITE 2	CP - 44	KIK GROUP STR 2 LVL 4 UNIT 13 LOT 4	ALEXANDERS UNSLIPPED
CALCITE 2	CP - 59B	FIGUEROA GROUP STR 3 LVL 1-2 UNIT 1	ALEXANDERS UNSLIPPED
CALCITE 2	CP - 4	TOLOK GROUP STR 1 LVL 1 UNIT 3	CAYO UNSLIPPED
CALCITE 2	CP - 51	KIK GROUP STR 2 LVL 4 UNIT 13 LOT 4	CAYO UNSLIPPED
CALCITE 2	CP - 6	TOLOK GROUP STR 1 LVL 1 UNIT 3	CAYO UNSLIPPED
CALCITE 2	CP - 27	PLAZA B LVL 1-2 UNIT 1	MOUNT MALONEY BLACK
CALCITE 2	CP - 62A	FIGUEROA GROUP STR 3 LVL 1-2 UNIT 1	MOUNT MALONEY BLACK
CALCITE 2	CP - 28	PLAZA B LVL 1-2 UNIT 1	TU-TU CAMP STRIATED
CALCITE 2	CP - 31	PLAZA B LVL 1-2 UNIT 1	TU-TU CAMP STRIATED
CALCITE 2	CP - 29	PLAZA B LVL 1-2 UNIT 1	NOT TYPED
CALCITE 2	CP - 32	PLAZA B LVL 1-2 UNIT 1	NOT TYPED
CALCITE 2	CP - 48	KIK GROUP STR 2 LVL 4 UNIT 13 LOT 4	NOT TYPED
VOLCANIC 1	CP - 50A	KIK GROUP STR 2 LVL 4 UNIT 13 LOT 4	BELIZE RED
VOLCANIC 1	CP - 56A	FIGUEROA GROUP STR 3 LVL 1-2 UNIT 1	BELIZE RED
VOLCANIC 1	CP - 59A	KIK GROUP STR 1 LVL 4 UNITS 1 & 9	BELIZE RED
VOLCANIC 1	CP - 60A	KIK GROUP STR 1 LVL 4 UNITS 1 & 9	BELIZE RED
VOLCANIC 2	CP - 70	FIGUEROA GROUP STR 3 LVL 1-2 UNIT 1	BELIZE RED
VOLCANIC 2	CP - 49	KIK GROUP STR 2 LVL 4 UNIT 13 LOT 4	BELIZE RED
VOLCANIC 2	CP - 63	FIGUEROA GROUP STR 3 LVL 1-2 UNIT 1	XUNANTUNICH BLACK ON ORANGE

Inventory of Thin Sectioned Sherds from Pacbitun by Petrofabric

PETROFABRIC	SHERD	CONTEXT	TYPE-VARIETY
CALCITE 2	PN - 14	NW TRANSECT MOUND 16 LOT 512-1	MOUNT MALONEY BLACK
VOLCANIC 1	PN - 8	NW TRANSECT MOUND 18 LOT 426-1	BELIZE RED
CALCITE 2	PN - 15	NW TRANSECT MOUND 33 LOT 479-1	GARBUTT CREEK RED
GRANITE	PN - 10	NW TRANSECT MOUND 61 LOT 442-1	CAYO UNSLIPPED
CALCITE 2	PN - 2	LOT 390 BURIAL STR 1 & 4	GARBUTT CREEK RED
CALCITE 2	PN - 3	LOT 390 BURIAL STR 1 & 4	GARBUTT CREEK RED
CALCITE 1	PN - 4	LOT 164 SOUTH OF BALLCOURT	MOUNT MALONEY BLACK
CALCITE 2	PN - 5	LOT 164 SOUTH OF BALLCOURT	ALEXANDERS UNSLIPPED
VOLCANIC 1	PN - 6	LOT 164 SOUTH OF BALLCOURT	PLATON PUNCTATE INCISED
CALCITE 2	PN - 7	LOT 177 STR 4 BASE OF STELA	MOUNT MALONEY BLACK
CALCITE 1	PN - 1	STELA 8 LOT 194	PABELLON MOLDED-CARVED
VOLCANIC 2	PN - 9	SW TRANSECT MOUND 60 LOT 401-1	PABELLON MOLDED-CARVED
GRANITE	PN - 13	SW TRANSECT MOUND 62 LOT 481-1	CAYO UNSLIPPED
GRANITE	PN - 12	SW TRANSECT MOUND 1 LOT 513-1	CAYO UNSLIPPED
CALCITE 2	PN - 11	SW TRANSECT MOUND 34 LOT 398-2	ALEXANDERS UNSLIPPED

Inventory of Thin Sectioned Sherds from Baking Pot by Petrofabric

PETROFABRIC	SHERD	CONTEXT	TYPE-VARIETY
CALCITE 1	BP - 37	CARACOL FARM MOUND 13	ALEXANDERS UNSLIPPED
CALCITE 1	BP 144	BALLCOURT STR L BC-4 L3	BELIZE RED
CALCITE 1	BP - 129	GRP 1 PLAZA 2 STR F UNIT 40 L2	CAYO UNSLIPPED
CALCITE 1	BP - 48	CARACOL FARM MOUND 2 L1	CHUNHITZ ORANGE
CALCITE 1	BP - 4	BEDRAN MOUND UNIT 2 L1 CACHE 22	DOLPHIN HEAD RED
CALCITE 1	BP - 42	BEDRAN MOUND UNIT 2 L1 CACHE 22	DOLPHIN HEAD RED
CALCITE 1	CP - 29	CARACOL FARM MOUND 13	DOLPHIN HEAD RED
CALCITE 1	BP 123	GRP 1 PLAZA 2 STR F WEST EDGE UNIT 32 L1	DOLPHIN HEAD RED
CALCITE 1	BP - 23	GRP 1 SOUTH BALLCOURT L1	DOLPHIN HEAD RED
CALCITE 1	BP - 54	NORTH CARACOL FARM MOUND 14 L1	DOLPHIN HEAD RED
CALCITE 1	BP - 131	GRP 1 PLAZA 2 STR F UNIT 35 L1	GARBUTT CREEK RED
CALCITE 1	BP - 135		GARBUTT CREEK RED
CALCITE 1	BP - 132	GRP 1 PLAZA 2 STR F UNIT 35 L1	MOUNT MALONEY BLACK
CALCITE 1	BP 122	GRP 1 PLAZA 2 STR F WEST EDGE UNIT 32 L1	MOUNT MALONEY BLACK
CALCITE 1	BP - 22	GRP 1 SOUTH BALLCOURT L1	TU-TU CAMP STRIATED
CALCITE 1	BP - 26	GRP 1 SOUTH BALLCOURT L1	TU-TU CAMP STRIATED
CALCITE 2	BP 139	BALLCOURT STR L BC-4 L3	ALEXANDERS UNSLIPPED
CALCITE 2	BP - 5	BEDRAN MOUND UNIT 2 L1 CACHE 22	ALEXANDERS UNSLIPPED
CALCITE 2	BP - 6	BEDRAN MOUND UNIT 2 L1 CACHE 22	ALEXANDERS UNSLIPPED
CALCITE 2	BP 125	GRP 1 PLAZA 2 STR F WEST EDGE UNIT 32 L2	ALEXANDERS UNSLIPPED
CALCITE 2	BP - 24	GRP 1 SOUTH BALLCOURT L1	ALEXANDERS UNSLIPPED
CALCITE 2	BP - 111	STR 193 UNIT 4 L1	ALEXANDERS UNSLIPPED
CALCITE 2	BP - 36	CARACOL FARM MOUND 2 L1	BELIZE RED
CALCITE 2	BP - 117	ATALAYA STR 2-3 UNIT 4 L1	CAYO UNSLIPPED
CALCITE 2	BP - 112	STR 193 UNIT 4 L1	CAYO UNSLIPPED
CALCITE 2	BP - 113	STR 193 UNIT 4 L1	CAYO UNSLIPPED
CALCITE 2	BP 71	STR E UNIT 7 L3	CAYO UNSLIPPED
CALCITE 2	BP 83	STR E UNIT 7 L4	CAYO UNSLIPPED
CALCITE 2	BP 85	STR E UNIT 7 L6	CAYO UNSLIPPED
CALCITE 2	BP 82	STR E UNIT 7 L4	DOLPHIN HEAD RED
CALCITE 2	BP - 108	STR 193 UNIT 4 L1	GARBUTT CREEK RED
CALCITE 2	BP - 103	STR 193 UNIT 4 L1	MOUNT MALONEY BLACK
CALCITE 2	BP - 104	STR 193 UNIT 4 L1	MOUNT MALONEY BLACK
CALCITE 2	BP - 75	STR E UNIT 7 L7	MOUNT MALONEY BLACK
CALCITE 2	BP - 134	GRP 1 PLAZA 2 STR C UNIT 44 L2	TU-TU CAMP STRIATED
CALCITE 2	BP - 133	GRP 1 PLAZA 2 STR F UNIT 35 L1	TU-TU CAMP STRIATED
CALCITE 2	BP - 106	STR 193 UNIT 4 L1	TU-TU CAMP STRIATED
GRANITE	BP 124	GRP 1 PLAZA 2 STR F WEST EDGE UNIT 32 L2	ALEXANDERS UNSLIPPED

GRANITE	BP 70	STR F SIDE E UNIT 5/6 BALLCOURT	ALEXANDERS UNSLIPPED
GRANITE	BP - 58	ATALAYA STR 1 UNIT 1 L2	CAYO UNSLIPPED
GRANITE	BP 140	BALLCOURT STR L BC-4 L3	CAYO UNSLIPPED
GRANITE	BP 141	BALLCOURT STR L BC-4 L3	CAYO UNSLIPPED
GRANITE	BP - 21	GRP 1 SOUTH BALLCOURT L1	CAYO UNSLIPPED
GRANITE	BP 74	STR E UNIT 7 L2	CAYO UNSLIPPED
GRANITE	BP 77	STR E UNIT 7 L5	CAYO UNSLIPPED
GRANITE	BP 142	BALLCOURT STR L BC-4 L3	DOLPHIN HEAD RED
GRANITE	BP 78	STR E UNIT 7 L5	DOLPHIN HEAD RED
GRANITE	BP 136	BALLCOURT STR L BC-4 L3	TU-TU CAMP STRIATED
VOLCANIC 1	BP - 57	ATALAYA STR 1 UNIT 1 L2	BELIZE RED
VOLCANIC 1	BP - 53	CARACOL FARM MOUND 2 L1	BELIZE RED
VOLCANIC 1	BP 126	GRP 1 PLAZA 2 STR F WEST EDGE UNIT 32 L2	BELIZE RED
VOLCANIC 1	BP 127	GRP 1 PLAZA 2 STR F WEST EDGE UNIT 32 L2	BELIZE RED
VOLCANIC 1	BP 128	GRP 1 PLAZA 2 STR F WEST EDGE UNIT 32 L2	BELIZE RED
VOLCANIC 1	BP - 30	CARACOL FARM MOUND 13	BENQUE VIEJO POLYCHROME
VOLCANIC 1	BP - 1	BEDRAN MOUND UNIT 2 L1 CACHE 22	PABELLON MODELED CARVED
VOLCANIC 1	BP - 31	CARACOL FARM MOUND 13	PLATON PUNCTATE INCISED
VOLCANIC 2	BP 143	BALLCOURT STR L BC-4 L3	BELIZE RED
VOLCANIC 2	BP - 2	BEDRAN MOUND UNIT 2 L1 CACHE 22	BELIZE RED
VOLCANIC 2	BP - 49	CARACOL FARM MOUND 2 L1	BELIZE RED
VOLCANIC 2	BP - 20	GRP 1 SOUTH BALLCOURT L1	BELIZE RED
VOLCANIC 2	BP 138	BALLCOURT STR L BC-4 L3	MOUNT MALONEY BLACK
VOLCANIC 2	BP 137	BALLCOURT STR L BC-4 L3	TU-TU CAMP STRIATED

Inventory of Thin Sectioned Sherds from Xunantunich by Petrofabric

PETROFABRIC	SHERD	CONTEXT	TYPE-VARIETY
CALCITE 1	XN - 13	STR A-1 79 BB/9.7039	DOLPHIN HEAD RED
CALCITE 1	XN - 24	SL22 STR 3 110 G19-0113243	GARBUTT CREEK RED
CALCITE 1	XN - 25	STR A-25 117 G/3.10752	GARBUTT CREEK RED
CALCITE 1	XN - 7	STR A-6 102 H/5-D2	MOUNT MALONEY BLACK
CALCITE 1	XN - 10	STR D-7 22 T/1-P01.11436	MOUNT MALONEY BLACK
CALCITE 2	XN - 14	STR A-25 116C/4.10968	ALEXANDERS UNSLIPPED
CALCITE 2	XN - 15	STR A-24 123 C/8.11386	ALEXANDERS UNSLIPPED
CALCITE 2	XN - 11	STR A-1 79 R/2.5400	DOLPHIN HEAD RED
CALCITE 2	XN - 28	SL22 STR 1 113 G-7.13251	GARBUTT CREEK RED
CALCITE 2	XN - 31	STR D-7 22 L/5.4708	MOUNT MALONEY BLACK
CALCITE 2	XN - 32	STR D-7 22 L/5.4708	MOUNT MALONEY BLACK
CALCITE 2	XN - 33	STR D-7 22 Q/4.4457	MOUNT MALONEY BLACK
CALCITE 2	XN - 36	STR A-24 123 A/10.11282	TU-TU CAMP STRIATED
CALCITE 2	XN - 38	STR A-24 123 A/8.11217	TU-TU CAMP STRIATED
GRANITE	XN - 37	STR A-24 123 C/4.11332	TU-TU CAMP STRIATED
VOLCANIC 1	XN - 1	STR A-4 12 A/1	BELIZE RED
VOLCANIC 1	XN - 5	STR A-24 123 A/10.11282	BELIZE RED
VOLCANIC 1	XN - 6	STR A-6 102 LL/3.15128	BELIZE RED
VOLCANIC 1	XN - 30	STR A-5 112 M/2.D1.13129	BELIZE RED
VOLCANIC 1	XN - 27	STR A-25 117 C/4.10606	BENQUE VIEJO POLYCHROME
VOLCANIC 1	XN - 3	STR A-1 79JJ47.5093	CHUNHITZ ORANGE
VOLCANIC 1	XN - 4	STR A-25 117G/B.10838	CHUNHITZ ORANGE
VOLCANIC 1	XN - 21	STR A-24 123 C/6.11353	CHUNHITZ ORANGE
VOLCANIC 1	XN - 23	STR A-1 79 JJ/40.15076	ZACATEL CREAM POLYCHROME
VOLCANIC 2	XN - 2	STR A-1 79U/10.3811	BELIZE RED
VOLCANIC 2	XN - 29	STR A-1 79 JJ/17.13095	BELIZE RED
VOLCANIC 2	XN - 20	STR A-1 79 BB/11.383542	BENQUE VIEJO POLYCHROME
VOLCANIC 2	XN - 22	STR A-1 79 AA/3.7002	ZACATEL CREAM POLYCHROME

Inventory of Thin Sectioned Sherds from Blackman Eddy by Petrofabric

PETROFABRIC	SHERD	CONTEXT	TYPE-VARIETY
CALCITE 1	BE - 14	A7 OP 16 A-2	NOT TYPED
CALCITE 1	BE- 15	A7 OP 16 A-2	DOLPHIN HEAD RED
CALCITE 1	BE - 13	A7 OP 16 A-2	GARBUTT CREEK RED
CALCITE 1	BE - 12	A7 OP 16 A-2	MOUNT MALONEY BLACK
CALCITE 2	BE - 1	B1 15 N-85 LEVEL 3	CAYO UNSLIPPED
CALCITE 2	BE - 2	B1 15 N-85 LEVEL 3	CAYO UNSLIPPED
CALCITE 2	BE -7	B1 15 N-85 LEVEL 3	CAYO UNSLIPPED
CALCITE 2	BE- 16	A7 OP 16 A-2	CAYO UNSLIPPED
CALCITE 2	BE - 4	B1 15 N-85 LEVEL 3	DOLPHIN HEAD RED
CALCITE 2	BE - 6	B1 15 N-85 LEVEL 3	DOLPHIN HEAD RED
CALCITE 2	BE - 9	B1 15 N-85 LEVEL 2	DOLPHIN HEAD RED
CALCITE 2	BE - 10	A7 OP 16 A-2	MOUNT MALONEY BLACK
CALCITE 2	BE - 8	B1 15 N-85 LEVEL 2	TU-TU CAMP STRIATED
CALCITE 2	BE - 17	A7 OP 16 A-2	TU-TU CAMP STRIATED
VOLCANIC 1	BE - 5	B1 15 N-85 LEVEL 3	BELIZE RED
VOLCANIC 1	BE - 11	A7 OP 16 A-2	BELIZE RED
VOLCANIC 1	BE - 3	B1 15 N-85 LEVEL 3	CHUNHITZ ORANGE

Inventory of Thin Sectioned Sherds from Ontario Village by Petrofabric

PETROFABRIC	SHERD	CONTEXT	TYPE-VARIETY
CALCITE 1	OV - 15	OVA -1 OP2A LEVEL 5	CAYO UNSLIPPED
CALCITE 1	OV - 12	ONA - 1OP2A LEVEL 5	DOLPHIN HEAD RED
CALCITE 1	OV -13	OVA - 1 OP2A LEVEL 5	DOLPHIN HEAD RED
CALCITE 1	OV - 1	OVA - 1 OP2A LEVEL 1	GARBUTT CREEK RED
CALCITE 1	OV - 11	OVA - 1 OP2A LEVEL 5	GARBUTT CREEK RED
CALCITE 1	OV - 9	OVA - 1 OP2A LEVEL 5	MOUNT MALONEY BLACK
CALCITE 2	OV - 4	OVA - 1 OP2A LEVEL 1	CAYO UNSLIPPED
CALCITE 2	OV - 14	OVA - 1 OP2A LEVEL 5	CAYO UNSLIPPED
CALCITE 2	OV - 2	OVA - 1 OP2A LEVEL 1	GARBUTT CREEK RED
CALCITE 2	OV - 3	OVA - 1 OP2A LEVEL 1	MOUNT MALONEY BLACK
CALCITE 2	OV - 6	OVA - 1 OP2A LEVEL 5	TU-TU CAMP STRIATED
CALCITE 2	OV - 8	OVA - 1 OP2A LEVEL 5	TU-TU CAMP STRIATED
VOLCANIC 1	OV - 7	OVA - 1 OP2A LEVEL 5	BELIZE RED
VOLCANIC 1	OV - 16	OVA - 1 OP2A LEVEL 5	BELIZE RED
VOLCANIC 1	OV - 10	OVA - 1 OP2A LEVEL 5	PLATON PUNCTATE INCISED
VOLCANIC 2	OV - 5	OVA - 1 OP2A LEVEL 1	BELIZE RED

Inventory of Thin Sectioned Sherds from Floral Park by Petrofabric

PETROFABRIC	SHERD	CONTEXT	TYPE-VARIETY
CALCITE 1	FP - 1	FPA1 OP 1-I-1	GARBUTT CREEK RED
CALCITE 1	FP - 2	FPA1 OP 1-I-1	MOUNT MALONEY BLACK
CALCITE 1	FP - 3	FPA1 OP 1-I-1	MOUNT MALONEY BLACK
CALCITE 2	FP - 4	FPA1 OP 1-I-1	ALEXANDERS UNSLIPPED
CALCITE 2	FP - 5	FPA1 OP 1-I-1	ALEXANDERS UNSLIPPED
CALCITE 2	FP - 6	FPA1 OP 1-I-1	CAYO UNSLIPPED
CALCITE 2	FP -7	FPA1 OP 1-I-1	CAYO UNSLIPPED
CALCITE 2	FP - 8	FPA1 OP 1-I-1	GARBUTT CREEK RED
CALCITE 2	FP - 9	FPA1 OP 1-I-1	GARBUTT CREEK RED
CALCITE 2	FP -10	FPA1 OP 1-I-1	MOUNT MALONEY BLACK
VOLCANIC 1	FP -11	FPA1 OP 1-I-1	BELIZE RED
VOLCANIC 1	FP - 12	FPA1 OP 1-I-1	BELIZE RED
VOLCANIC 1	FP -13	FPA1 OP 1-I-1	CHUNHITZ ORANGE
VOLCANIC 1	FP -14	FPA1 OP 1-I-1	CHUNHITZ ORANGE
VOLCANIC 1	FP - 15	FPA1 OP 1-I-1	BENQUE VIEJO POLYCHROME

Inventory of Thin Sectioned Sherds from El Pilar by Petrofabric

PETROFABRIC	SHERD	CONTEXT	TYPE-VARIETY
CALCITE 1	YAXOX - 10	278-026 14279 LVL 1 UNIT 2N 12E	ALEXANDERS UNSLIPPED
CALCITE 1	PILAR - 1	272-220 14230 LVL 1 UNIT 22S 20E	CAYO UNSLIPPED
CALCITE 1	PILAR - 3	272-220 14230 LVL 1 UNIT 22S 20E	DOLPHIN HEAD RED
CALCITE 1	YAXOX - 13	278-026 14269 LVL 1 UNIT 6N 10E	DOLPHIN HEAD RED
CALCITE 1	BACAB - 12	281-021 13344 LVL 6 UNIT 22B 16E-16	GARBUTT CREEK RED
CALCITE 1	YAXOX- 14	278-026 14342 LVL 2 UNIT 4N 10E	GARBUTT CREEK RED
CALCITE 1	ZOTZ - 9	272-005 17225 LVL1 ZOTZ-NA	GARBUTT CREEK RED
CALCITE 1	PILAR - 4	272-220 14230 LVL 1 UNIT 22S 20E	MOUNT MALONEY BLACK
CALCITE 1	YAXOX -2	278-026 14257 LVL 1 UNIT 14N 10E	MOUNT MALONEY BLACK
CALCITE 1	YAXOX - 4	278-026 14342 LVL 1 UNIT 4N 10E	MOUNT MALONEY BLACK
CALCITE 2	BACAB - 3	281-021 13173 LVL 2 UNIT 22N 14E-10	ALEXANDERS UNSLIPPED
CALCITE 2	BACAB - 4	281-021 13405 LVL 7-8 UNIT 22N 12E-5	ALEXANDERS UNSLIPPED
CALCITE 2	PILAR - 2	272-220 14351 LVL 1 UNIT 12S 15E	ALEXANDERS UNSLIPPED
CALCITE 2	ZOTZ - 6	272-005 17225 LVL1 ZOTZ-NA	ALEXANDERS UNSLIPPED
CALCITE 2	BACAB - 5	281-021 13077 LVL 1 UNIT 22N 30E-7	CAYO UNSLIPPED
CALCITE 2	YAXOX - 15	278-066 14354 LVL 1 UNIT 24N 24E	CAYO UNSLIPPED
CALCITE 2	YAXOX - 11	278-026 14246 LVL 1 UNIT 12N 12E	CAYO UNSLIPPED
CALCITE 2	ZOTZ - 5	272-005 17228 LVL1 ZOTZ-NA	CAYO UNSLIPPED
CALCITE 2	ZOTZ - 7	272-005 17228 LVL1 ZOTZ-NA	CAYO UNSLIPPED
CALCITE 2	BACAB - 11	281-021 13261 LVL 8 UNIT 24N 22E-9	GARBUTT CREEK RED
CALCITE 2	YAXOX - 17	278-006 14386 LVL 1 UNIT 30N 20E	GARBUTT CREEK RED
CALCITE 2	ZOTZ - 8	272-005 17228 LVL1 ZOTZ-NA	KAWAY IMPRESSED
CALCITE 2	BACAB - 7	281-021 13068 LVL 1 UNIT 22N 28E-11	MOUNT MALONEY BLACK
CALCITE 2	BACAB- 8	281-021 13068 LVL 1 UNIT 22N 28E-11	MOUNT MALONEY BLACK
CALCITE 2	BACAB - 1	281-021 13078 LVL 1 UNIT 30N 20E-9	TU-TU CAMP STRIATED
CALCITE 2	BACAB - 2	281-021 13083 LVL 1 UNIT 28N 20E-17	TU-TU CAMP STRIATED
GRANITE 1	BACAB - 6	281-021 13068 LVL 1 UNIT 22N 28E-11	CAYO UNSLIPPED
GRANITE 1	YAXOX - 8	278-026 14236 LVL 1 UNIT 12N 12E	CAYO UNSLIPPED
GRANITE 1	YAXOX - 9	278-026 14256 LVL I UNIT 12N 10E	CAYO UNSLIPPED
GRANITE 1	YAXOX - 1	278-026 14246 LVL 1 UNIT 12N 12E	MOUNT MALONEY BLACK
VOLCANIC 1	BACAB - 10	281-021 13042 LVL 6 UNIT 22N 32E-3	BELIZE RED
VOLCANIC 1	BACAB - 9	281-021 13045 LVL 6 UNIT 32N 20E-2	BELIZE RED
VOLCANIC 1	PILAR - 5	272-220 14306 LVL 1 UNIT 10S 22E	BELIZE RED
VOLCANIC 1	YAXOX - 16	278-006 14410 LVL 1 UNIT 14N 20E	BELIZE RED
VOLCANIC 1	YAXOX - 3	278-026 14273 LVL 1 UNIT 4N 8E	BELIZE RED
VOLCANIC 1	YAXOX - 5	278-026 14276 LVL 1 UNIT 2N 9E	BELIZE RED
VOLCANIC 1	YAXOX - 6	278-026 14299 LVL 1 UNIT 6N 12E	BELIZE RED
VOLCANIC 1	YAXOX - 7	278-026 14299 LVL 1 UNIT 6N 12E	BELIZE RED
VOLCANIC 1	ZOTZ - 4	272-005 17225 LVL 1 ZOTZ-NA	BELIZE RED
VOLCANIC 1	ZOTZ -2	272-005 17231 LVL 1 ZOTZ-NA	BELIZE RED
VOLCANIC 1	ZOTZ - 3	272-005 17227 LVL 1 ZOTZ-NA	BELIZE RED - MARTINS INCISED
VOLCANIC 1	YAXOX - 12	278-026 14256 LVL 1 UNIT 12N 10E	CAYO UNSLIPPED
VOLCANIC 2	ZOTZ - 1	272-005 17225 LVL 1 ZOTZ-NA	GALLINERO FLUTED

Appendix B – Data Collection Form

SHERD:

SITE:

CONTEXT:

COMPLEX:

GROUP:

TYPE-VARIETY:

DIMENSIONS:

Thickness

⃝ Description

RIM
IN-TURNED.....
OUT-TURNED.
STRAIGHT......
FLATTENED ...
WIDENED......
TAPERED.....
NOTE...........

BASE
RING..........
FLAT.........
CONCAVE....
DIMPLED...
ROUNDED..
OTHER.......
NOTE.........

FEATURES
HANDLE(S)..
LUG(S) ....
SPOUTS......
LIP.............
FEET...........
NOTE. ....

SURFACE
HARSH....
ROUGH....

BODY
SPHERE..........
OBLATE...........
ELONGATE.....
SEGMENT......
HEMISPHERE..
CONE..........
CYLINDER ....
CARINATION.

DECORATIVE FORMING
BURNISH....
INCISION....
EXCISION....
MOULDED..
APPLIQUE ...
IMPRESSED.
STRIATED...
PUNCTATE...
MODELED ...
RIDGED.......

Notes on Surface Treatment & Decoration:

SLIP COLOUR:
int ext
Red
Orange
Black
Brown
Cream

DECORATION LOCATION

RIM NECK HANDLE TOP 3RD MIDDLE 3RD BOTTOM 3RD

INSIDE......
OUTSIDE...

SKETCH:

FABRIC DESCRIPTION

THIN-SECTION (Y/BLANK)

PETROFABRIC

HARDNESS
VERY HARD
HARD..........

FRACTURE
CONCHOIDAL.......
EVEN...............
IRREGULAR.......
HACKLY............

BODY COLOUR | MUNSELL | DESCRIPTION
EXTERIOR...........
EXT MARGIN......
CORE................
INT MARGIN.......
INTERIOR...........

FABRIC NAME

	INCLUSION #.	COLOUR......	FRACTURE: CONCHOIDAL....	NON-DIAGNOSTIC...	CLEAVAGE	PERFECT........	GOOD.........	POOR........	PARTING.....	LUSTRE: METALLIC.....	VITREOUS.....	OILY.......	EARTHY.....	PEARLY.....	DIAPHENEITY: TRANSPARENT.....	TRANSLUCENT.....	OPAQUE......	SECTILITY: SECTILE......	NON-SECTILE.....	HARDNESS: VERY SOFT....	SOFT......	HARD......	VERY HARD...	MAGNETISM: STRONG.......	WEAK.......	NONE........	ACID REACTION: STRONG.......	WEAK.......	NONE........	IDENTIFICATION.....	FREQUENCY (%).....	SORTING: VERY WELL.....	WELL......	MODERATE.....	POORLY.....	GRAINSIZE: GRIT.......	VERY COARSE SAND	MEDIUM SAND	COARSE SAND...	FINE SAND....	ROUNDNESS: ANGULAR.....	SUBANGULAR...	SUBROUNDED...	ROUNDED.....	WELL-ROUNDED...
1																																												
2																																												
3																																												
4																																												
5																																												
6																																												
7																																												
8																																												
9																																												
10																																												

NOTES

DATE (dd/mm/yy) / /

www.ingramcontent.com/pod-product-compliance
Lightning Source LLC
Chambersburg PA
CBHW051305270326
41926CB00030B/4734

* 9 7 8 1 4 0 7 3 0 5 9 3 6 *